Carole Lombard

Carole Lombard
A Bio-Bibliography

Robert D. Matzen

Bio-Bibliographies in the Performing Arts, Number 4

GREENWOOD PRESS
New York • Westport, Connecticut • London

Library of Congress Cataloging-in-Publication Data

Matzen, Robert D.
    Carole Lombard : a bio-bibliography / Robert D. Matzen.
        p.   cm.—(Bio-bibliographies in the performing arts, ISSN
    0892-5550 ; no. 4)
    Includes index.
    ISBN 0-313-26286-1 (lib. bdg. : alk. paper)
    1. Lombard, Carole, 1908-1942. 2. Lombard, Carole, 1908-1942—
Bibliography. 3. Motion picture actors and actresses—United
States—Biography. I. Title. II. Series.
PN2287.L625M35   1988
791.43'028'0924—dc19
[B]   88-15429

British Library Cataloguing in Publication Data is available.

Library of Congress Catalog Card Number: 88-15429
ISBN: 0-313-26286-1
ISSN: 0892-5550

First published in 1988

Greenwood Press, Inc.
88 Post Road West, Westport, Connecticut 06881

Printed in the United States of America

The paper used in this book complies with the
Permanent Paper Standard issued by the National
Information Standards Organization (Z39.48-1984).

10 9 8 7 6 5 4 3 2 1

Copyright Acknowledgments

The author and publisher are grateful to the following for granting the use of
material:

"Every Actor Should Take at Least One Week's Whirl at Publicity" by Carole
Lombard appearing in The Hollywood Reporter—18th Anniversary Issue. © The
Hollywood Reporter—18th Anniversary Issue.

Every reasonable effort has been made to trace the owners of copyright materials
in this book, but in some instances this has proven impossible. The publisher will
be glad to receive information leading to more complete acknowledgments in subsequent printings of the book and in the meantime extend their apologies for any
omissions.

For Trudy

Contents

Illustrations

Preface

Carole Lombard crossed the Indianapolis Airport runway at 4 a.m. against a stinging frozen wind, and she barely retained the strength to climb the steps of the waiting DC-3 and walk inside. She was thirty-three years old, and the previous day tens of thousands of people had braved a Midwest January day to catch the slightest glimpse of her. Many had pledged hundreds of dollars or more for an autograph or the privilege of shaking her hand.

Sitting there on the plane in complete exhaustion, Lombard clung to the notion that in less than twenty-four hours she would snuggle securely in the arms of her husband, Clark Gable, the most desired man in America. She was a beautiful blonde with a tennis-lean body. She earned upwards of a quarter of a million dollars a year, lived on a picturesque ranch in the country, and no matter how she looked at it, no matter how tired she was or how badly her eyes burned for sleep, Carole Lombard knew she had it all.

Fifteen and a half hours later on a bleak Sierra Nevada mountaintop, steam and smoke mingled over charred flesh. The creamy skin, the golden blonde hair, the dynamic personality, all gone. Bodies and pieces of bodies lay everywhere and around them, mountain timber blazed in a funeral pyre. Above, on a sheer cliff, a huge oil stain marked the spot where the DC-3 had impacted after glancing off a lower ledge. Bodies and wreckage, blood and snow, and the end of an era.

"Do you believe in God?" she had recently asked a startled columnist, out of the blue. (See reference source no. 122, page 154). This from a Carole Lombard who trumpeted no religion and attended church only at weddings and funerals. Was she pondering her own fate? The fate of a world plunged in war? No one can be sure, but the question suddenly gained an eerie significance as shockwaves of the crash rippled outward through the darkness.

Hollywood mourned Carole Lombard as it had never mourned one of its own: with profound silence. No ballyhoo. No Busby Berkeley send-off. *This* death hurt too

much.   President Franklin Roosevelt eulogized her, the
Senate honored her with a moment of silence, and Carole
Lombard passed into legend.
    Like many others on this earth, she lived brilliantly
and died young.   She made her mark on-screen as a comedienne. Off-screen she was an experimenter hooked on sensation; a saber-witted conversationalist, a sensuous woman
who very rarely wore a bra, a sports addict, a social butterfly, a feminist, a prankster who loved to show off dead
things.
    Indeed, it is the *real* Carole Lombard--the living,
breathing, energetic human being--that spawned the bulk of
the legend because of the sublime uniqueness of the woman
and her personality.
    "I *love* everything I do," Lombard said with typical
animation in 1938.   "I'm intensely interested in and
enthusiastic about everything I do, *everything*. No matter
what it is I'm doing, no matter how trivial, it isn't
trivial to me.   I give it all I got and I love it." (See
source no. 087, page 148).
    Photoplay reporter Adele Whitely Fletcher summed up
the experience of interviewing Lombard this way: "All
Carole's conversation should be underscored for emphasis,
with some words and sentences doubly underscored.   Only
the presses won't work that way!" (See source no. 079).
    "She's a shot in the arm," enthused writer Elizabeth
Wilson, "she's a cold shower, she's a double martini,
she's a whiff of smelling salts, she's a Dashiel Hammett
story, she's the Best." (See source no. 140).
    The allusions here are important as they capture a
Lombard that is shocking, strong, unconventional, and com-
plicated--not exactly the traits that the America of the
1930s held dear in women.   Elizabeth Wilson interviewed
Lombard more than any other Hollywood reporter and knew
she had become one of Carole's close friends when the star
began insulting her regularly, and delighted in it when
Wilson fired insults back in return.
    Carole Lombard was the product of a Hollywood far out
of step with the real world yet created by that world.
Hollywood in its Golden Era was one brightly lit, hurly-
burly, Technicolor exception to a drab, Depression-devas-
tated America. And in this *anything goes* environment,
Carole Lombard possessed the protean ability to be viewed
in different ways by different people.
    When inspired to do so, she could lounge in a bubble-
bath and emerge in a cloud of perfume, step into silk
lingerie and melt in a man's arms like a sleepy kitten.
Or she could pull back her hair, dangle a Camel from her
lips, pour a beer and let loose a string of profanity that
separated men from boys.   In point of fact, she possessed
the foulest mouth Hollywood had ever heard, and she used
it with panache.   "We used to call Carole the *profane
angel*," said director Mitchell Leisen, "because she looked
like an angel, but she swore like a sailor...She was the
only woman I ever knew who could tell a dirty story with-

out losing her femininity. (See source no. 024).

Lombard fit Hollywood like Lana Turner fit her sweaters: provocatively. The stars of the Golden Era came from different places--from as near as Hollywood High, and as far as Tasmania--creating room for many personality types and many outlooks. Still, Lombard was *too* innovative and therefore set apart, branding herself a *new woman*, forcing the world to re-examine its values and its sense of propriety.

As a Hollywood businesswoman, Lombard became the ultimate publicity hound of the decade, appearing in more fan magazine articles than any other star, and often gracing the covers of those magazines. She mugged for cameramen at every opportunity, and issued press releases that sounded important even though they usually weren't. In short, Carole Lombard was the very definition of flamboyance and wore it like a shimmering gown, to the height of perfection.

Actor Ralph Bellamy said in a recent letter, "It was a delight to work with Carole. She was herself in everything she did and she glowed." As an actress, she appeared in fifty-two motion pictures in twenty-one years, and she epitomized the Hollywood dream by paying her dues, overcoming adversity, and finally achieving recognition for hard-earned skills.

Lombard claimed Mack Sennett as her comedic influence, yet she created a wholly original style that was copied by her peers and remains today as the benchmark by which all other comedic actresses are measured.

"Carole had a quality which is rare," said Desi Arnaz in his autobiography, *A Book* (William Morrow and Co., 1976). "You can count the women who have had it on the fingers of one hand. Carole, while doing the wild antics of a clown...could make you laugh, and yet at the same time make you want to go to bed with her."

To the men of Hollywood, Carole Lombard was the Holy Grail of the female sex; men fell in love--or lust--with her routinely, often causing her great pain. Still she adored being chased, wherever it led. All part of her grand experiment at living.

Writer/director Garson Kanin met her when he was twenty-eight. He recalls that "like everyone else who ever came into contact with Carole Lombard, I fell...She was everything I had always wanted a girl to be: beautiful, funny, talented, imaginative, able, warm, dear, and no-nonsense. I found myself touching her at every possible opportunity, and when those opportunities did not arise, I invented some." (See source no. 021).

In a 1986 interview with this writer, Robert Stack related that when he was fourteen, Lombard stayed at his family's home at Lake Tahoe and he also fell in love: "She was my idealization of what a young boy would *dream* of seeing; a movie star. She was it. There she was, in a bathing suit coming out of the water. Beautiful! And I just kind of looked with pop-eyes."

Although Stack was a mere teenager at the time, Lombard treated him with rare respect. "She was terribly *aware*," he said. "She treated the boy as you would the man. She never downplayed to me as a kid."

Sensual and sensuous, profane, sensitive, vain about her beauty, extravagant, raucous, feminine, visceral. All these were Carole Lombard.

"Do you believe in God?" The question lingers. How unlike her to speak of God; how very like her to be curious, and to question.

Carole Lombard possessed so much energy, questioned so much and as a result became so much the expert at living, that by the time she died on that jagged, frozen mountaintop as World War II began, her death personally affected everyone who was anyone in Hollywood. And at 7:22 p.m. on January 16, 1942, Hollywood lost not only its most dynamic personality, but its Golden Era as well.

This volume is an attempt at assembling all known information sources regarding Lombard. And it is more. It is a biography, a filmography, and a sampler of Carole Lombard's wit, her interviews, her writins, and her life and times. It can be asserted that Lombard profoundly affected the cinematic style of all screen comediennes, changed the perception of starlets as prima donnas and second class citizens, and stood at the vanguard (inconspicuously, as history records such contributions) of the struggle of women to achieve equality, in and out of Hollywood. Hopefully, this book will confirm these assertions and contribute toward posthumous recognition of a truly notable star.

Acknowledgments

Books are never created alone. With this in mind, I doubt that I could have completed this project without the timely and generous assistance of Susan Marie Rice, Ann Toth, John Metzger, Guy Tomcik, and Tom Johnston. Robert Stack allowed me into his home and shared with me cherished memories of Carole Lombard. Ralph Bellamy, Olivia de Havilland, and James Stewart took the time to respond to my queries. In addition, I would like to thank the following people for their contributions to this book: Carol Brack, Marilyn Brownstein, Ken Fornof, Julie Glynn, Janet Gonter, Debbie Greenbank, Pam Groff, Beverly Hebelka, Bea Hurwitz, Jim Jeneji, Ray Jones, Tichi Wilkerson Kassel, Mike Mazzone, John McElwee, Jeffrey S. Mintz of the National Film Information Service, Stephen Sally, James G. Stewart, Tony Thomas, Jim Trupin, Esther Tucker, Gary Vaughn, Elizabeth Welch, the staff of the Margaret Herrick Library of the Academy of Motion Picture Arts and Sciences, and the staff of the National Archives. Lastly, I wish to thank my wife, Debra, for her continued support and assistance.

1. Biography

Carole Lombard began life on October 6, 1908 as Jane Alice Peters in a spacious two story frame house at 704 Rockhill Street in Fort Wayne, Indiana. Her parents, Frederick Peters and Elizabeth Knight Peters, came from similar upper-middle class backgrounds. The Peters family had brought the first washing machine to America, and it was in a washing machine factory accident that young Fred received injuries that left him with a game leg, a limp, and led to serious headaches that would plague him for the rest of his life. No-nonsense Elizabeth, known as "Bessie" to her friends, was pretty and sophisticated and had borne her husband two sons, Frederick and Stuart, before Jane's arrival in 1908.

For the Peters family and ultimately for America, life would never quite be the same after Jane made her first appearance. What an appearance it was; huge, pleading blue eyes, blonde hair, a round face. And from the start she possessed vast amounts of energy that her mother appreciated and her father didn't.

Jane's earliest years were entirely normal. For buddies she had Freddy, who was six years her senior, and Stu, who was much closer in both age and temperament. As soon as she could walk, Jane tagged along after her big brothers, and gaining acceptance in their eyes became her number one preoccupation.

From birth through age five, Jane enjoyed her one and only silver spoon period, marked by two large, omnipresent families, both of which spoiled her. She went to the theatre once a week to see moving pictures, enjoyed the luxury of dancing lessons, and generally lived quite a happy childhood in this close-knit family setting.

But in 1914, halfway across the world came the drama of Sarajevo, the assassination of an archduke and for Europe, war. Unexpectedly, like some worldwide epidemic, war even touched the far-flung corner of Fort Wayne, Indiana. In October, 1914, for reasons never clearly documented, Bessie Peters packed up both clothes and children, and seceded from her union with Fred Peters. Four-fifths of the Peters family headed west by train, hit San Francisco

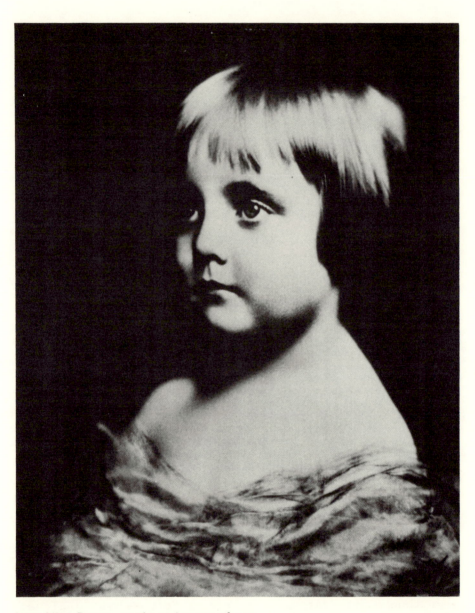

Jane Alice Peters, at about 4 years of age.

Jane Peters, age 8.

a glancing blow and ended up in Los Angeles, where Bessie fell in love with sunny days, balmy nights, palm trees, and the hot Santa Ana wind. Old friends transplanted from Fort Wayne would keep her company. Fred and Stu missed their playmates, but they had each other. Jane had never made close friends, so she didn't miss them when she moved. Instead, she remained completely involved with her brothers, her heroes. "The trouble was," she said years later, "I always had the feeling that I couldn't keep up." (See reference source no. 002, page 132).

Nor could she easily keep up with the family's subsequent moves from apartment to apartment around Los Angeles, drifting ever farther westward toward a seemingly inevitable brush with the burgeoning new capital of moving pictures, Hollywood. Living so close to this magic town made new schools and new neighborhoods tolerable, and it didn't seem to bother Jane that she never stayed in any one place long enough to drop anchor and make real friends. She was content that it was always her and Freddy and Stu.

A glimpse of the Jane Peters of this era can be seen through the eyes of Delmer Daves, noted Hollywood writer and director. Daves lived on Wilshire Boulevard when the Peters did, and was just the right age, sixteen, to pal around with Freddy and Stu.

Daves found the ten year old Jane a real bother because she was, after all, only a girl, and "not an attractive girl; she was scrawny. I didn't pay much attention to her, really. She teased me about that, too, when we--as they say--grew up. Carole, with her four letter words. She said, 'You fucking bastard, you never even looked at me!'" (See reference source no. 039).

With the boys almost grown and Jane enrolled in both elementary school and the Nolkes Dramatic School for Girls, Bessie had more free time for friends, among whom were Al and Rita Kaufman, who had relatives in the film business. When the Peters visited the Kaufmans, Stu and Jane would go next door to see an esteemed Kaufman neighbor, Benny Leonard. Leonard was known as the Ghetto Wizard and had owned the lightweight boxing championship of the world for the past three years. A tough-talking New Yorker who stood all of five foot five, Benny possessed iron fists and a classic style, and he didn't just decision opponents, he destroyed them. "No performer in any art has ever been more correct than Leonard," Haywood Broun stated at the time. "He stands up straight like a gentleman and a champion and is always ready to hit with either hand."

This was the legend Jane Peters met at the age of twelve. He was a great man, a somebody; the first real, successful somebody Jane had ever known.

Before long the Ghetto Wizard taught Jane how to box in the Leonard style. She had already been able to handle herself in scraps with both boys and girls. From here on in, it pretty much became a slaughter, as if she were

walking around with two loaded six-guns. All her life she
would boast about her ability to fistfight, as taught by
the Ghetto Wizard back on those mean streets of L. A.

Before long she learned just how lucrative the fight
game really was.   This lesson came on that same fateful
block where lived the Kaufmans and Benny Leonard. One day,
Allan Dwan was walking toward the Kaufman home when he
glanced into Leonard's backyard and saw "a cute-looking
tomboy...knocking hell out of the other kids."   (See
source no. 022).

Jane was then plucked off the street by Allan Dwan to
work for three days on the film *A Perfect Crime*, portraying the hero's tomboy little sister.   It wasn't a
challenging role, considering that each morning tomboy
Jane left two hero/brothers of her own back at home.   Of
the experience of acting in a Hollywood motion picture,
Allan Dwan said, "she ate it up." (See source no. 047).

When it was over, Jane reluctantly got on with her
life, looking on *A Perfect Crime* as a novelty, a fringe
benefit of living near exciting Hollywood.   By now she
possessed some degree of her mother's intuition, and while
Jane's desire to become an actress now took shape and
solidified, she seemed to sense she still had a long way
to go.

As Jane Peters became a teenager, the Peters family
changed residences yet again, this time to a house on
Manhattan Place, scant blocks from the bustling Paramount
Studios. Jane attended Virgil Junior High and then Fairfax High School in the heart of the film community.   At
Fairfax High, Jane's natural athletic ability--which she
channeled into tennis and the girl's track team--coupled
with her flair for drama to earn her instant popularity.
Of course, being pretty helped. In fact, the tomboy Delmer Daves described, the one in *A Perfect Crime*, had so
emphatically changed that she was selected as Fairfax
High's May Queen of 1924.

At the May Day pageant, Jane was spotted by Alfred
Reeves, who worked for the great Charlie Chaplin. Reeves'
clandestine mission of the day was to watch out for un-
knowns who might fit the bill as Chaplin's leading lady in
the soon to be filmed United Artists production, *The Gold
Rush*.

Jane Peters captured Reeves'attention with shimmering
blue topaz eyes, a creamy complexion, and especially with
the hypnotic way she seemed to draw his, and everybody
else's, gaze.   Reeves made a beeline for Jane's mom and
arranged a meeting for the following day between Jane
Peters and one Charles Chaplin, perhaps the most important
man in Hollywood.

The results of that meeting weren't immediately evident. On the contrary, from the start her chemistry with
the intense thirty-five year old Chaplin just wasn't
right. He did grant her a screen test which she eagerly
made, but *The Gold Rush* eventually became the highwater
mark of eighteen year old Georgia Hale's career, not Jane

Peters'.

Charlie Chaplin's interest did, however, lead the Fox
Studio to put out feelers and when Vice President and
General Manager Winfield Sheehan took one look at radiant
Jane Peters, bingo!

Jane signed her name on the dotted line of a standard
one year Fox contract as soon as she turned sixteen in
October, 1924. Her first action as a Fox player, taken
with Bessie's approval, was to quit school. What good was
a high school diploma to a young girl in Hollywood, anyway? She wasn't out to become a Fox secretary; she wanted
Fox stardom.

Her second action as a contract player was calculated
to help the odds. Fox executives had told her flatly that
Jane Peters wasn't the kind of name one built a career
around. A Jane Peters was a mother in middle America with
a brat under each arm. No big problem. Jane had always
favored the name Carol, after Carol Peterson, one of her
tennis buddies from junior high. She coupled this name
with Lombard, after Bessie's close friend, esteemed Los
Angeles banker Harry Lombard.

Jane Peters then became Carol Lombard, and eagerly
reported for bit parts in *Gold and the Girl* and *Dick
Turpin*. She decided early on that hanging out on the
male-dominated backlot sets was great fun. All the actors
and stunt men treated her very well, and she began to
learn that those swear words Freddy and Stu gagged on so
clumsily through the years could actually serve a purpose
when used in the proper context. When one of the grips
needled her, she would throw a "Kiss my ass!" or a "Piss
off!" back at him, and the guys on the set loved it, and
her.

But life on the sets was only half the fun. In the
evenings she would take some of her weekly salary and skip
on down Western Avenue to Wilshire and the Ambassador
Hotel, specifically to the Ambassador's downstairs
nightclub, the Cocoanut Grove. There she would hang out
with kids her own age, and very soon, in the Grove's
exotic environment, the suddenly self-confident, bubbly
Carol Lombard became a flapper and went wild. Dancing,
smoking, driving, nipping at bootlegged whiskey. "It
was," said one of Carol's contemporaries, "a good time to
be young."

Carol enjoyed her life as a Fox starlet to the hilt,
although as her first year neared completion, the Fox
braintrust decided that Carol Lombard, although pretty
enough, just wasn't quite leading lady material. She
clearly didn't have what it took in terms of star quality
or notable talent, and Fox decided to allow her contract
to lapse without renewal.

In a matter of months Carol Lombard's promising
career was sputtering to a stop. She abandoned the Grove,
stopped dating, and spent more time at home with Bessie,
crying on her mother's shoulder.

At this lowest point in her young life, she received

a much-needed lucky break.   Somehow, John Barrymore, the great Warner Brothers star, got hold of a Carol Lombard still and decided to test her for *Tempest*, his upcoming Russian Revolution epic.

She passed this test and Fox immediately treated her with more respect.   They dug up a new project, *Early to Wed*, a comedy, and penciled it into the schedule with Lombard as the female lead.

With John Barrymore's help, Carol arose from the depths of depression and returned to her second home, the Cocoanut Grove.   Life became one long party again, with dancing and dating, dating and dancing.   She had already appeared in five films, a number that so recently seemed pitifully small but now formed a foundation on which to build, especially when she could soon add *Tempest* and *Early to Wed* to the list.

Then, in October, 1925, Lombard suffered through the most traumatic experience of her life.   It started out innocently enough as a joyride through the Hollywood Hills in a friend's roadster and ended in an accident that shattered the windshield "like a fireworks explosion," as Carol later phrased it. (See source no. 021). She turned her face away, felt a storm of slicing glass pelt her. She looked down at herself; blood, glass were everywhere.

In the hospital emergency room an hour later, she requested that a cosmetic surgeon examine a deep gash in her left cheek and another beside her eye.   The specialist told her that she would need stitches--without an anesthetic. He explained how certain muscles work to maintain the appearance of the face. Allow those muscles to relax during surgical repair, and you'd have a real catastrophe upon healing; something only Lon Chaney would appreciate. But certain procedures could be performed in surgery, like the removal of damaged tissue, and with the application of ointments after the operation, it might not turn out too badly in the end.   The most important item, he stated bluntly, was her complete cooperation, no matter how great the pain and discomfort.   And it would indeed be rough, and take many weeks, with no guarantee as to the results.

Afterward, for the teenager, the flapper, life was over, despite the doctor's assurances that the operation had gone well.   Her eighteenth birthday passed without fanfare, and it was obvious to her mother and brothers that Carol had given up.

Weeks later, hope returned when the bandages were removed and Carol was handed a mirror. A scar cut diagonally across her left cheek, but was less than an inch and a half long.   One end, the end pointing toward the top of her ear, was tiny and might completely fade.   The other end, pointing toward her nose, held less promise. It was indented like a misplaced dimple, and discolored to a reddish brown. Otherwise, both cheeks matched, and she could count herself one fantastically lucky girl.

More weeks in bed followed, first in the hospital, then at home, protecting that precious piece of craftsmanship on her cheek.   But now she had fighting spirit.   Now she asked her mother to bring her books on cosmetology and photography.   She was hungry for information on covering up that scar, and for filming around it once she went back to work.

One afternoon in the spring of 1926 she pronounced herself fit to meet the world.   She interviewed at various studios, and executives wondered where she had been, why they hadn't seen her on the screen. She was ill, she said. But *ill* meant any number of problems in Hollywood.   They wondered if she was a dope addict, alchoholic, or had had an abortion. Wearing an exaggerated bob that partially covered her cheek, and applying the best makeup she could find, she hid her scar so well that few learned the truth unless she decided to tell it. A solid year of rejection followed until the spring of 1927 when she got a tip that Mack Sennett Comedies was hiring a replacement in its bevy of slapstick Bathing Beauties. Carol quickly made inquir- ies. It was an opportunity that likely would not come twice.

Carol arranged an interview and found that Mack Sennett already knew of her accident and her scar, and he didn't care in the least.   Like the Keystone Kops of a decade earlier, his popular Bathing Beauties were his trademark, and quite a breakthrough in the popular cinema. Sennett presented the sex-starved post-Victorian world some much needed titillation by stripping his girls down to the essentials and leaving little to the imagination.

Carol was assured by Sennett that her face was fine and her body even better. At fifty dollars a week, twen- ty-five more than she made at Fox before the accident, Carol had herself a job. Sennett would later boast that he had *discovered* Lombard, an obviously innacurate claim. He did, however, *rescue* her when she was down and out, something just as important. (See source no. 034).

During the next year and a half, Carol appeared in more than a dozen Sennett two-reelers, and here the Screw- ball Queen of the movies learned timing, and how to react like a good second banana when the top banana threw a pie or turned on a raging water hose.   For teachers she had Mack Sennett himself plus former vaudevillian and Sennett veteran Mack Swain, and midget-sized slapstick actress Daphne Pollard.   Then there was the big girl of the group whom Sennett placed among the Beauties because, "There's only one thing visually funnier than a fat girl, and that's a fat girl in a bathing suit." (See source no. 036). Her name was Madalynne Fields, dubbed "Fieldsie" by Carol, and they quickly became inseparable best friends.

While Carol plugged along for Sennett, she freelanced in her spare time, taking anything that would enlarge her resume. She appeared in a cheapie Rayart Pictures release called *The Divine Sinner*. After that came a role in *Power* with William Boyd and Joan Bennett for the Pathe Studios, low billing in *Me, Gangster*, directed by Raoul Walsh for Fox, and the second female lead in Pathe's *Show Folks*.

When released in October, 1928, reviewers hated *Show Folks*, with its musical score and dialogue section, but the magazine *Picture Play* said, "Carol Lombard, a very pretty blonde, is worth watching." Only, Carole Lombard didn't happen to agree. During a projection room screening of the film, she sat there stunned, thinking her performance "miserable," and afterward ran off in tears. (See source no. 051). Twenty minute silent comedies were one thing; feature films, with sound, were something else again. Carole realized the difference and quickly became her own harshest critic.

As luck would have it, *Show Folks* had an impact on one important person: the new Pathe Studios head, Joseph P. Kennedy, the father of a later U. S. president and two senators. Evidence points to the fact that popular silent-era actress and Sennett graduate Gloria Swanson advised the already interested Kennedy of Lombard's potential, and this led to a frank exchange between the scarfaced girl and the rich Irishman, in Kennedy's office.

Later that afternoon Carol walked away with a breathtaking four hundred dollar a week contract with Pathe Studios that immediately launched her into a string of feature films. At the same time she squeezed in three more Sennett shorts before that studio finally turned belly-up in 1929.

The death of Sennett's company came at an opportune moment, freeing Carol for a couple of prospectively big projects. First, Howard Hughes saw a photo of Lombard (a la Barrymore) and asked Joe Kennedy if he could make a test of her. The twenty-three year old whiz kid Hughes had been laboring on his epic *Hell's Angels* for two years with a Swedish leading lady, and when sound made its bombastic entrance into the film world, Hughes faced the unpleasant task of reshooting all dialogue with an American actress who could be labeled a "Hughes discovery." After her screen test, Lombard and Hughes began a liason of several months that ended when eighteen year old Jean Harlow appeared on the scene and riveted Hughes's attention. Dollar signs lit up in his eyes, and he knew he had found his brand new star.

In the wake of the *Hell's Angels* disappointment there appeared another ray of hope. No less than Cecil B. De-Mille approached Joe Kennedy to make a film for Pathe using that studio's own Carol Lombard. DeMille proclaimed he would make the film *Dynamite* his explosion into the dynamic new sound era. He had been the man who gave the world *The Ten Commandments* and *King of Kings*, and was known to be a nice guy to his intimates but an autocrat on the set. DeMille would chew out an actor or actress unmercifully, with no regard for feelings or who might be watching. He wasn't Lombard's kind of guy. She would blow a line and laugh at herself nervously, and the intimidating DeMille would growl something to the effect that this wasn't the damned Keystone playpen, and you'd better shape up right this minute!

She didn't, and she was fired from a motion picture production for the only time in her career. (See source no. 036). She had received plenty of publicity for this particular role, and the axe-like execution really smarted. Never again would she presume that she could appear nonchalant before the camera; never again, after the clapboard clapped, would Carol Lombard seem anything but professional. Six years later, after she had garnered her fair share of accolades for what critics said was a surprising amount of acting ability, she felt confident enough to look back on her early years as a starlet and admit she was so uncomfortable in front of a camera that she didn't even know what to do with her hands.

"I was always hanging onto something. If there wasn't a handy chair, or a railing, I'd drape both hands over one hip and wait for the director to have hysterics." (See source no. 109). Problems like these would continue to plague her, but with a sharp mind, photogenic face and knockout body, Carol would never want for work.

It was now the spring of 1930. The Depression had crunched America a few months earlier, and she counted herself lucky not to be standing in a breadline somewhere with all those poor joes who couldn't make their own breaks or control their own destinies.

She got a part in the Paramount film *Safety in Numbers* and promptly signed a seven year Paramount contract starting at three hundred seventy-five dollars a week. A considerable sum for a talent as yet unproven. Her first film under contract to the studio, *Fast and Loose*, became important in Lombard's history for quite an offbeat reason. Somebody in the advertising department goofed when printing up the posters for the film's November, 1930 release. Somehow, *Carol* became *Carole*. When told of the error, she beefed at first, then looked at the poster long and hard and finally admitted she liked it. "I think the e made the whole fuckin' difference," she later told Garson Kanin. (See source no. 021).

It was magic, that name, pure magic, and Carole well knew it. She grew friendlier by the day in Paramount's confines, and very soon hired old buddy Madalynne Fields to act as her secretary and advisor. The one-two punch of the closing of Mack Sennett Comedies and the 1929 Depression had left Fieldsie both dazed and unemployed. She knew Carole was being *too* nice, that Carole was doing her a huge favor, but Carole always maintained she couldn't function without Fieldsie's guidance.

Within months of her arrival at Paramount, Carole began a friendship with Horace Liveright, the founder of Boni and Liveright book publishers, and the producer of such successful plays as *An American Tragedy* (1926) and *Dracula* (1927). Liveright had been ruined by the stock market crash of October, 1929, and when he moved west, Paramount boss Adolph Zukor hired him out of pity to be a studio story researcher.

Although forty-three years old to Carole's twenty-

one, Liveright became an ardent, and gallant, pursuer on
the lot.   The mature Lombard had always found herself
drawn to older men and she said of Liveright, "I admired
him enormously.   I liked everything about him.   I liked
his style.   I liked his tastes, his hobbies, his friends,
the things he did and the way he did them.

"He taught me things, lots of them. He opened doors
to me.   He brought out the best in me.   And," she said
sadly, "I would have been positively ill if he had ever
kissed me." (See source no. 086).

Their breakup came swiftly and the once-powerful man
soon left Paramount, returned to New York, married on the
rebound, and died in 1933 at the age of forty-six. Carole
never spoke directly of Liveright to the press, although
he apparently asked her to marry him. "We were tempera-
mentally unsuited," she explained in 1931.   "I knew if I
told him goodbye I'd almost die. I did." (See source no.
086).

Not that she still wasn't man crazy.   She would fall
in love with great regularity in the next three years.
The first of these great loves came along as Carole prepared for the Herman Mankiewicz drama *Man of the World*.
She was working for the first time with an actor, William
Powell, whom the title Man of the World fit like a glove.
Powell was a Broadway veteran who had appeared in thirty-
four silent films before making his mark as popular private eye Philo Vance in three recent motion pictures.   By
the end of 1930, he was Paramount's top leading man, and
soon, Bill Powell and Carole Lombard were an item.

Their second teaming, in *Ladies' Man,* would introduce
Lombard to Kay Francis, a former Powell girlfriend and a
rising starlet every bit as unorthodox and opinionated as
Lombard.   The friendship established here, although not
close, would last until the end of Carole's life.

The surprise engagement of Carole to Bill Powell
occurred as she began work on her next film, *I Take This
Woman* with Gary Cooper.   *I Take This Woman* wasn't much,
just another weepy drama, but Lombard could take great
satisfaction in *Variety*'s review of June 16, 1931: "A few
more performances like this from Carole Lombard and
Paramount will have a new star on its list...Miss Lombard
ought to advance rapidly from this point."

Advance she did, straight to a makeshift altar in
Bessie Peters' new (rented) Beverly Hills mansion at 619
Rexford Drive, where Carole Lombard and William Powell
were married on June 26, 1931 before a small assemblage of
friends.

The ensuing Powell-Lombard marriage immediately revealed its obvious flaws, since Powell traveled in elite,
intellectual circles while Carole bummed around much of
the time, giggling with Fieldsie, salting every sentence
with a "shit" or a "fuck."

A Hawaiian honeymoon followed the ceremony, with Carole
contracting either the flu or food poisoning that laid her
low for the duration.

Back in Hollywood, she began work on the film *No One Man* and then wham, landed back in bed with vague complaints that turned out to be pleurisy. This new malady, piled on top of her previous afflictions, confused and frightened the robustly active Carole Lombard, who either couldn't or wouldn't connect this string of illnesses with her unhappiness at married life.

Carole finished *No One Man*, then didn't work for months.

It was a hell of a life for a former flapper, a woman who considered herself mature in some ways, but who still never really wanted to grow up. Living first in her husband's fashionable Havenhurst Drive apartment, then in a spacious two story house on North Beverly Drive, wearing the best clothes, eating the best food, and most importantly, rubbing elbows with the elite of Hollywood society might have tickled most women to death. But Carole Lombard wasn't most women, and this wasn't Lombard's kind of a life to lead.

She did, however, form an alliance with Bill's agent, Myron Selznick, brother of David O., and suddenly *the* agent one wanted to have if one was a Hollywood contract player. Bill had just found this out very quickly when Myron Selznick snagged him an astounding six thousand dollar a week contract at Warner Brothers. Another Selznick client, Kay Francis, also jumped from Paramount to Warner Brothers at this time, taking with her a generous new long-term deal.

At Bill's urging, Carole grudgingly sold her soul to the Selznick Agency, and the results were swift and awesome: a renegotiated, more solid contract with Paramount plus a hefty raise. "Every time I make a picture," she said, "I feel it's the last time. When Fox didn't pick up my option a while back, I wasn't even surprised. But when Paramount actually gave me the dough I asked for--well, I felt kind of weak. I can't get rid of the feeling that none of it's real." (See source no. 002).

Selznick had held up the affable bosses at Paramount as if he were Jesse James and they a bank. Consequently, the relationship between star and management became temporarily strained. After a brief strike over a proposed loanout to Warner Brothers that fell through, Carole made the weak *Sinners in the Sun* with Chester Morris. During production of this film, excessive red ink forced a shakeup at Paramount that brought Emanuel Cohen to power as studio head. Cohen decided the best way to utilize his very expensive, largely unproductive and unmemorable lady star Lombard was to loan her out to the first studio that winked in his direction. He offered her around like a shiny new penny and like lightning, she got shoved in Columbia's direction to work for Harry Cohn, the most despised of movie moguls. Those who worked for Cohn referred to him as "Harry the Horror," although the tough-as-nails Lombard stood up to him immediately and entered into Hollywood's tiniest minority group: the friends of

Harry Cohn.

Soon after her arrival at Columbia, Carole met writer Robert Riskin, a literary genius who had created the screenplay for her new film, *Virtue*. Sparks flew from the start, and her wounded marriage to Bill Powell was doomed.

Of Bob Riskin, Carole told Garson Kanin, "You always try to get in solid with the son of a bitch by playing his game. So when I went around with Bob Riskin...I started in reading books. I don't mean just bullshit. I mean book books. Aldous Huxley and Jane Austen. Charles Dickens. William Faulkner. Because Bob, he was an intellectual...And I felt I had to keep up. You know how it is." (See source no. 021).

For the duration of her stay at Columbia, which included the film *No More Orchids* as a follow-up to *Virtue*, Carole had to stash Bob Riskin, since Bill Powell wasn't working and would frequently show up on her sets unannounced.

Back at Paramount, a studio still deeply in debt, Carole was given the part of a nice-girl librarian in love with a con man in the film *No Man of Her Own*. Cast opposite her was the thirty-one year old, suddenly very hot Clark Gable of MGM.

No Man of Her Own, the only Lombard-Gable screen teaming, is an amusing and interesting film, notable for its early 1930s raciness. The smug Gable meets naive Lombard the librarian and asks her to climb a ladder to fetch him a book. She climbs and he roguishly peers up her skirt, clearly impressed. Later, Carole strips down to bra and panties, and Gable shows up. She hurries into slinky lounging pajamas, and Gable surveys her like a driver with a new race car. "Mmmm," he growls, "pajamas." Their scenes together sizzle although Lombard acknowledged no attraction between them.

Her next assignment proved quite a comedown as she endured the production of the awful *From Hell to Heaven*, followed by special degradation at the hands of director Victor Halperin during the making of the film *Supernatural*. (See Chapter 4). Carole was by now growing especially bitter at Paramount's choice of roles for her. While she was busy sparring with the likes of an inept Victor Halperin, Paramount actresses like Marlene Dietrich and Claudette Colbert were enjoying great prosperity.

Carole played a cameo role in the excellent, grade A production of *The Eagle and the Hawk* with Fredric March, but her career was going nowhere--as proven by her next dud of a film, *Brief Moment* with Gene Raymond--and her personal life was a mess. On the fourth of July, 1933, Lombard and Powell agreed to divorce. The next day, she and Fieldsie drove eastward over the Nevada line to Reno, divorce capital of the United States, and established a residence there for six weeks.

That's where columnist Louella Parsons caught up with Carole, breathless from a speedboat ride, for her first interview in self-imposed exile. To Carole's credit, it was an honest exchange containing no smoke-screens. "I have worked hard to achieve what small success I have made," she stated, "and I simply can't bear to give it all up." She said that Bill wanted to retire from the screen and travel; travel would mean retirement for Carole as well. (From *The Hollywood Reporter*, 31 July 1933).

In August, in the court of Carson City, Lombard was granted a divorce in six minutes' time. As she pushed her way through a sea of male admirers she quipped, "It's like a stag party." (From *The Hollywood Reporter*, 21 August 1933). Behind the gaiety was great pain. Robert Stack, at whose house Carole was staying, recalled that Bill Powell had sent an affectionate letter to Carole. "The tears streamed down her face," said Stack. (See source no. 035).

She returned to Hollywood, where her next film was *White Woman*, a steamy jungle epic filmed on Paramount sound stages. During its production, Robert Riskin took Carole to the Silver Slipper nightclub in Los Angeles for a romantic tete a tete. Here, on this night, Lombard confounded Riskin by falling head-over-heels in love with America's "Singing Romeo," crooner Russ Columbo. The feeling was mutual, and Columbo pursued her like a hound after a fox. They began dating, became lovers. One columnist said, "Everybody who ever saw them together knew that he adored her." (See source no. 002).

Russ Columbo's name was big in 1933; much bigger, in fact, than Lombard's. This was the time of the Battle of the Baritones, a spurious rivalry built up between Columbo and Bing Crosby purely for the sake of publicity.

"He was a handsome guy," Crosby told talk show host Joe Franklin, "and he had a warm, ingratiating personality. He could sing, and he was a good musician. He played wonderful violin... We were great pals."

On the radio, Columbo and Crosby sounded so similar that only a rivalry could define their individual characters. George Burns kidded, "They both sang exactly alike and I couldn't understand it. Two guys, singing alike, and they're both stars! I sang entirely different and couldn't get any place." (See source no. 038).

While embroiled in this new romance with Columbo, Carole finished *White Woman* at the end of September, 1933, and saw it released a rapid seven weeks later. Critics hated it but happily, her film held much more promise.

The steamy, passionate *Bolero*, co-starring the new sensation George Raft, would ultimately bring Carole more critical attention than anything she had done to date. It was a story that roughly paralleled Raft's own life: common man with great ambition reaches the height of fame and success. Raft was handsome, tough, and likeable; if Russ Columbo hadn't been keeping her so busy, Carole would have taken far greater notice of Paramount's new tough guy.

After *Bolero*, Carole made the musical comedy *We're Not Dressing* with Bing Crosby, and she then, thanks to her rare camaraderie with Harry Cohn, lucked into the role at Columbia that would alter the course of her career and

Carole Lombard and William Powell at Santa Anita Racetrack, 1933.

thus her life: *Twentieth Century*.

Twentieth Century was a richly pedigreed film, written by Ben Hecht and Charles MacArthur (*The Front Page, Scarface*), and to be directed by Howard Hawks. John Barrymore was a natural for the lead role of Oscar Jaffe, the bellowing, egocentric Broadway producer who makes a star out of store clerk Lily Garland, played by Lombard.

In the speedy five week shooting schedule, Carole learned more about acting, more about herself, than she had in the past ten years put together. Under the tutelage of Hawks and Barrymore she *became* Lily Garland exactly as ordered, strutting with her nose in the air like a genuine prima donna, bouncing around defiantly braless, growling at people, mocking them--playing her role from the gut as she had never done before. When the production wrapped, Barrymore stunned Carole by calling her "probably the greatest actress I have ever worked with." (See source no. 036).

Unfortunately for Harry Cohn and Columbia, the film stalled at the box office despite glowing reviews. Still, Lombard wasn't bothered because she felt she had finally found herself as an actress.

"All the time I was making seventeen flops in a row," Carole said with a cold grip on reality, "I was scared to death they were going to call my bluff before had a chance to really learn something about this business. There is no one else on the screen who has had more consistently bad pictures than I." (See source no. 109).

Her next film was *Now and Forever*, a formula vehicle featuring six year old Shirley Temple and co-starring Gary Cooper. During the making of this film, the death of nineteen year old Miss America-turned-actress Dorothy Dell in a car crash profoundly affected both Carole and Russ. (See source no. 098). Parallels between Dell and Lombard-- from blonde hair to the fact that Dorothy bore scars from an earlier auto accident--didn't escape Carole's attention. To Columbo, Dell was an ex-lover whose memory haunted him, and in the wake of the tragedy, Lombard and Columbo decided to marry sometime in 1935.

Less than three months after Dell's fatal accident, Carole was already experiencing vague feelings of trepidation when she received a phone call saying that Russ had been shot. By the time she reached Good Samaritan Hospital, Columbo was dead at the age of twenty-six of an accidental gunshot wound to the eye. (See Chapter 4).

Lombard would never completely recover from Columbo's death, although she tried to disguise her suffering by adopting a new, bolder facade of madcap gaiety. She resumed work in a cliched MGM gangster film called *The Gay Bride*, and then returned to Paramount for her next film, *Rumba*, with George Raft. At the same time she made a pet project of redecorating the home she had leased the previous October as a means of shaking up her miserable life. Located on the winding residential western end of Hollywood Boulevard at 7953, the modest two story house had a

back yard big enough that she could start accumulating
pets and, eventually, entertain on a grand scale. She
redecorated this new home in a fury of concentrated activity as she set about the task of cleansing herself of
Russ's mjemory. Basically, it worked. She filled her
evenings haggling over colors, patterns and furniture
while spending her days at Paramount in the company of
George Raft, working on *Rumba*. Now alone, Carole craved
Raft's strength, support, and amorous attentions.
      "I truly loved Carole Lombard," George Raft stated
bluntly, later in his life. (See source no. 045).   In
1934, Lombard and Raft briefly became an item, and Carole
would later slyly identify George as the most talented
lover she had ever known. His flame was not, however,
eternal. It turned brightly for a short while, then faded
from sight, and he and Carole parted as friends.
      Soon she entered her party phase, throwing theme
bashes such as the *hospital party*, with waiters dressed as
doctors and supper served on operating tables, and the
hillbilly party, with a complete barnyard motif.   She
culminated this period with *the* social event of her life,
perhaps the most famous, talked-about, remembered party
in Hollywood history as she rented the entire Venice
Amusement Pier at Oceanside Park for one evening and
invited all of Hollywood to come have fun at her expense.
Lombard officially proclaimed that the Venice Pier party
was her swan song as a hostess, that she would now concen-
trate once again on her career after a much-needed six
month layoff.
      Back at Paramount, continued financial troubles led
to the insertion of German immigrant director Ernst
Lubitsch as general production manager. Lubitsch was
something of a gambler who liked Carole Lombard as a
talent. He trusted his instincts about a comedy script
called *Hands Across the Table*, and redesigned it with
Lombard in mind. To direct the film, he chose ambitious
young Mitchell Leisen at Carole's urging. Leisen had been
her friend since they had briefly worked together on the
film *Dynamite*, and of late Leisen had shown real promise
behind the camera, directing five films in the past two
years. As Lombard's co-star, Lubitsch drafted twenty-six
year old Fred MacMurray, big band saxophonist and, more
recently, a Paramount contract player just starting out.
MacMurray didn't know acting and he didn't know comedy,
but he was tall and boyishly handsome, and Lubitsch sensed
in him great potential.
      MacMurray found his first day of working with Carole
Lombard an eye-opening experience: "That evening I went
to see Lilly, who later became my wife, and she said,
'Well, how did it go with Carole Lombard?' I said, 'I
have never heard such profanity from anybody, man or
woman.' Lilly said, 'Other than that, what's she like?'
I said, 'She's wonderful.'" (See source no. 004).
      To say that Lubitsch had instant, unflappable confi-
dence in *Hands Across the Table*, its cast and crew, would

be erroneous.   Two weeks into production,   Lubitsch suffered a full-fledged anxiety attack and called Lombard   to
his   office. He wanted to cancel the entire project.   The
script was weak.   The director hadn't done comedy, nor had
Carole's co-star.

Lombard   took charge,   insisting that both Leisen and
MacMurray would   be fine.   She called in a script doctor
who made   some last minute screenplay changes,   and   the
production went ahead.

Of Carole's work in *Hands Across the Table*, film historian James Robert Parish said,   "Mitchell Leisen   worked
directorial wonders with her,   transforming previously im-
posed mannered comic acting into nonchalant breeziness."
(See source no. 027).

Upon release, the film proved a success and *Photoplay*
went so far as to call MacMurray "a grand   teammate"   for
Lombard.   The London *Times* offered rare praise for the two
leads and their handling of dialogue: "It is as if each
phrase was was only thought of the moment it was uttered."
Hands Across the Table wouldn't be a top grosser--although
it made   money--but it set Lombard on a new course   at
Paramount while at the same time establishing the career
of the young Fred MacMurray.

It was   during this period,   in 1935,   that Carole
helped save the career of tennis star Alice Marble,   who
was wasting away in a tuberculosis sanitorium at   age
twenty.   The empathic Lombard heard of Marble's plight
from tennis teacher Elinor Tennant and felt inspired to
sit down and write a moving letter, guarding her anonym-
ity, in which she explained how she had nearly lost her
career in the auto accident.   "Doctors told me I was
through," wrote Lombard, "but then I began to think I had
nothing to lose by fighting, so I began to fight.   Well--I
proved the doctors wrong.   I made my career come true,
just as you can--if you fight." (See source no. 039).

With strength gleaned from this letter, Alice Marble
began fighting back.   In 1936, Carole sat in the front row
of the audience as Alice won the California singles title
in straight sets.   She then marched eastward and won the
U. S. championship at Forest Lawn.   This was the start of
a torrid streak of success for Alice, who won three more
U. S. titles as well as three Wimbledon mixed doubles
titles, two doubles titles, and the Wimbledon singles
title in 1939. Carole watched Alice's career blossom with
pride.   She bankrolled a new wardrobe for Marble, and
often picked up her tabs--something that confounded the
tennis ace.   "Every time I tried to pay her back she said
Oh shit, forget about it! She was always embarrassed when
people wanted to thank her.   So whenever I won a championship I'd give her a silver tray.   I must have given her
twenty-five over the years, and she treasured them." (See
source no. 039).

Carole watched Alice's career blossom with pride and
no small degree of envy.   She was a "very good" tennis
player according to Marble, in fact the best woman player

Carole Lombard and Cesar Romero at the White Mayfair Ball, 1936.

in Hollywood.   At heart she may well have given up
everything to trade places with the tennis pro.   "I play
tennis now two and three hours a say," said Carole.   "I'm
working harder at it than I have ever worked at anything."
She smiled, adding, "And am I getting good." (See source
no. 089).

By 1936, Lombard was happily single and dating Cesar
Romero, among others.   She had also become an outspoken
critic of the institution of marriage, espousing beliefs
that seemed radical at the time, and perspicacious now,
when viewed with hindsight.

"In these times we are in a state of confused
changes," she said with conviction.   "From our gropings
will come a new and better order of things...We don't know
what to do with marriage today; we know something is
wrong.   We know it is due to conflict between the old
ideas men had toward women, and the changed status of
women."   (See source no. 074).

She believed that women should be free to pursue
careers whether married or not.   "It may be hard, at
first, for a man to adjust himself to a woman's independence," said Lombard.   "But--perhaps in spite of them-
selves--men respect an independent woman.   Instead of
jealousy and possessiveness, love can be based on a natural trust and honor." (See source no. 074).

In this frame of mind, Carole served as hostess for
the annual ultra-formal White Mayfair Ball, held on
January 25, 1936 at the Victor Hugo on Rodeo Drive.   It
was on this remarkable night, when all the women were
asked to wear white and Norma Shearer showed up in scar-
let--infuriating Lombard--that Carole fell in love with a
slightly drunk Clark Gable, forming a relationship that
would endure for the rest of her life.

Her supervision of the White Mayfair was proof of her
continued popularity among the Hollywood social set, yet
her career was again leveling off. She pondered the script
for a new film, *The Princess Comes Across*, and found it
decidedly weak because of an over-reliance on mystery.
She informed the studio that she would do the film only if
a gag writer punched it up into the status of a comedy
with serious overtones, rather than the other way around.
This concession was made.

"I've never fought unless I honestly believed I was
right," she felt compelled to say, "and that the thing I
was fighting for was really important." (See source no.
053).   Important enough that she alienated close friend
George Raft.

Raft was set to play the film's male lead but withdrew before shooting began. For the record he stated that
he disliked Carole's preferred director of photography,
Ted Tetzlaff, because Ted "gave Carole all the good
shots." Off the record he resented Lombard's meddling;
the way she changed the script and diminished the importance of his role.

Raft gave Paramount an "It's either him or me" ultima-

tum regarding Tetzlaff.   He knew full well that Carole
would never dismiss her favorite cameraman;   Raft himself
said,   "Carole was wholly generous,   always seeing to it
that people she knew or felt sorry for   worked as extras.
If they didn't work, she wouldn't go on the set."   (See
source no. 045).
     Carole stuck behind her cameraman rather than her   ex-
lover,   as predicted,   and as a result,   the film needed a
leading man.   Fred MacMurray was called upon as a   replacement,   since MacMurray had proven he could play comedy. Consequently, *The Princess Comes Across* became a second moderately successful teaming for the pair. *Moderately successful*.   The blockbuster,   breakthrough film still
eluded her, although it was inching closer with every day,
every breath.
     At Universal Studios,   a new project, *My Man Godfrey*,
was causing great interest,   especially after Universal
secured the services of William Powell from MGM,   where he
moved after his expensive agreement with Warner Brothers
had failed to work out.   Powell was asked if he could
think of an appropriate co-star.   His response was immediate: Carole Lombard.
     Universal granted Powell's wish disdainfully since
Lombard had rarely shown herself to be an audience favorite.   She was sent the script--about a rich man in hiding
who works as a butler for a houseful of zanies--and realized immediately that her ex-husband had let her in on a
goldmine.
     Goldmine indeed.   As with *Twentieth Century*, Lombard
took the ball and ran with it, breaking new ground in
acting, proving for the first time that a woman could perform the same kind of surrealist comedy as, say, the Marx
Brothers.   Her ethereal performance in the role of Irene
in this benchmark film of a genre soon being labeled
screwball,   set a standard that many tried to copy,   never
with complete success.
     Two years later she would remark,   "Irene in *Godfrey*
was,   I'd say, the most difficult part I ever played. Because Irene was a complicated and, believe it or not, essentially a tragic person." (See source no. 087).
     Perhaps this was why the Constance Bennetts and Irene
Dunnes never quite captured that Lombardian screwball
quality: they didn't see the humanity in the characters
they were portraying; just the nuttiness.   Lombard did see
it,   and America saw it,   and for the first time in her
career Carole Lombard was a household word.   Up to this
point,   she had relied on a zany reputation based on contrivance;   now she found an opportunity to let her talent,
hard-earned over the past dozen years, do the talking.
The result was an Academy Award nomination as Best Actress.   Finally, she was on her way.
     With her career rising and her relationship with
Clark Gable growing deeper, Lombard vacated her beloved
Hollywood Boulevard showplace in favor of a brick and
stucco tudor-style house at 609 St.   Cloud Road in se-

cluded, ultra-chic Bel Air. Hidden behind a dense growth of shrubbery and an electrically-controlled gate, it was a place she could meet Gable, who was then separated from his second wife, in complete privacy.

Like the house she had just left, her St. Cloud home was a showplace, beautiful to look at, with more room now for both pets and parties. She put this new house in order during a layoff from Paramount that lasted several months, then returned to work on a film called *Swing High, Swing Low*, an extravagant musical comedy/drama to co-star the ever more popular Fred MacMurray.

Carole learned a lesson in humility upon the film's completion, when she attended a sneak preview with Gable, Mitch Leisen, and two others in Long Beach in early March, 1937. When Lombard and Gable were spotted--both stars nearing the height of their popularity--the audience grew raucous, edgy, and all too eager to please. Carole related, "I went to a showing of the first rough cut of *Swing High, Swing Low* in a small college town. In the tragic scenes, where I screwed up my face to cry (I can't help it if I look that way when I cry), the audience laughed. When I really turned it on and emoted, they howled. It was heartbreaking. I felt like crawling under the seats and losing myself among the gum and other use-less things." (See source no. 127).

All drove down in one car, and Natalie Visart, Leisen's guest, recalled, "Mitch had done a beautiful, quiet, little scene where Carole sits down on her bed and slowly takes off her stockings, and starts to cry...On the way home, Carole and Mitch were close to tears because the audience had laughed at that scene. They both loved it, but they were determined to remove it...I have always thought it was a pity, because that scene showed the exquisite quality Carole had just a little bit better than anything else she ever did." (See source no. 004).

"That was the legacy of her success in *My Man Godfrey*," said Mitch Leisen. "People wouldn't accept the change from the comedy of the early scenes to the really terrific emotion she put over later." (See source no. 104).

As much as Carole regretted the cutting of that scene, she could still take satisfaction in the fact that *Swing High, Swing Low* wound up being Paramount's biggest moneymaking film of the year, a certain sign that Lombard now possessed the star power to draw in audiences on the strength of her name alone.

At this point, life was treating her very well. Thanks to Myron Selznick she was the highest paid woman in Hollywood, earning $150,000 per film, and she was learning to hunt ducks on long, arduous expeditions to Mexico with Clark Gable.

And then suddenly, at the beginning of June, 1937, at a moment when Hollywood had let its guard down, twenty-six year old Jean Harlow died.

To her friends and co-workers, to anyone who had ever

watched a Jean Harlow movie, it was as if one of their own children had been taken from them and murdered. It was too cruel a thing, too inhuman that a woman so young, a movie star so full of *life,* could be so carelessly removed from the world.

Harlow's death was very much a personal tragedy for Lombard. She had grown close to Jean through Clark Gable, and through Bill Powell, who had been Jean's companion for two years. Now Harlow's was another name to add to a list that included Dorothy Dell and Russ Columbo. All well short of thirty years of age. Deep down, Carole sensed that she too might not live that long a life. It was the flamboyant ones who died young, "in full bloom," as she put it. (See source no. 081). And Carole could identify flamboyance when she saw it, even in herself.

Following Columbo's death, Lombard's hatred of funer- als had achieved phobic proportions, yet she forged on, filled with dread, at Gable's side on Wednesday, June 9 when Jean Harlow was laid to rest at Forest Lawn of Glendale.

When it was over, Carole told pallbearer Gable that when *she* died, she envisioned a far different send-off. There was no room for doubt about this; she wanted no such spectacle, no such song-filled funeral service, no such collection of friends and enemies, reporters and photog- raphers to see her off. She told him to keep it digni- fied, short and sweet, and that then she would be at peace.

The death of Jean Harlow coincided with the withering of Carole's ties to Paramount, where she had only one pic- ture yet to make. She had recently signed a three year deal with Selznick International worth over a half a mil- lion dollars. This contract with Selznick resulted mainly from Carole's desire to play the role of Scarlett O'Hara in Selznick's hot property, *Gone With the Wind*, a project still two years away.

In the meantime, David Selznick created a comedy, *Nothing Sacred*, specifically to suit her screwball talents. Made soon after his landmark *A Star is Born*, the two films ended up looking a lot alike, given that both were directed by William Wellman, photographed by W. Howard Greene, shot in two strip Technicolor, and both starred Fredric March. Both were attacks on existing in- stitutions; *A Star is Born* revealed Hollywood as a flesh market following the theme, "You're only as good as your last picture," while *Nothing Sacred* circled over pompous New York City like a buzzard over a dying rabbit. *A Star is Born* told its story with tragedy; *Nothing Sacred* made its points through comedy and in both films, irony ruled. Audiences didn't necessarily plug into all of Selznick's intended cynicism, but both films scored as critical and boxoffice successes, and Lombard's popularity soared.

She then returned to Paramount one last time to make *True Confession*, another screwball comedy which told the story of Helen Bartlett, a habitual liar of a housewife who confesses to a murder she didn't commit.   To Carole, *True Confession* looked like a sure thing.   It read well, and she had long admired screenwriter Claude Binyon's work at Paramount.

Much to Binyon's credit, he wouldn't hold the experience of making *True Confession* against Carole Lombard. He had good reason to, since singlehandedly she ruined his efforts.   True, she looked better than ever in this film, and Fred MacMurray played her frayed, loveable husband with a yeoman's zeal.   But there was something unlikable about the essense of Lombard's character, and the flaw wasn't difficult to pinpoint: How could the audience root for a compulsive liar? In *My Man Godfrey* she had played a naive but good-hearted girl, in *Nothing Sacred* a regretful liar with plenty of conscience, and in *True Confession* Carole tried to take this character and her shtick one step further, except that here she crossed the line into bad taste.

The making of *True Confession* offers an insightful look into the mind of Carole Lombard, pointing up the fact that by now she exercised perhaps too much control over her films, enjoyed too much say-so about casting, and offered too many opinions about scripts.

Her budding megalomania first showed itself when she noticed that one of the minor roles was perfect for John Barrymore, except that it was much too small and would have to be built up. She put Binyon to work on it, argued for Barrymore with the Paramount brass, and got him.

"There's Lombard fighting for the underdog again," the brass would say, and Madalynne Fields would inevitably blanch when she heard such comments. "You don't understand Carole at all," Fieldsie would tell anyone who made an assumption like this.   "To her there are no underdogs." (See reference source no. 033).

Carole insisted that Barrymore be given equal billing behind herself and Fred MacMurray, and *True Confession*'s advertising showed the Great Profile to prominent advantage.

Unfortunately, so does the film, where Barrymore's scenes seem entirely out of place in the briskly paced screwball atmosphere--as if they were spliced in from a different film--and they serve as testimony to the bind in which Lombard placed Binyon, and to the way she unwittingly sabotaged her own project.

On the other hand, Lombard displayed in *True Confession* a sort of reckless energy that directors loved.   The climax of the film was shot at Lake Arrowhead in the mountains, and called for Carole to swim long stretches in icy late summer Arrowhead waters. More than that, she had to stay in those icy waters and recite dialogue with Fred MacMurray.   When it was over, she dragged herself out of the lake and fell unconscious on the shoreline.   A consulting doctor scolded director Wes Ruggles for subjecting a woman to such conditions. Later, Lombard would confound the Paramount publicity department by making them swear not to use this story in any way, shape, or form.

As 1937 wore on, Carole seemed to be wearying of the burden of a steady stream of comedies. "I had to struggle for years to do comedy," she said. "But I don't think I was at the top when I was merely an insipid ingenue, and I don't agree that I'm so proficient in comedy as I can be in straight drama. It's my goal, professionally. Otherwise I want a sane private life. That's why I look at those so-called glamour yarns as more of a handicap than a help. Fun's fun, in its place. I don't laugh always, though." (See source no. 110).

In her constant scheming to appear as Scarlett O'Hara in the ultimate straight drama, *Gone With the Wind,* Lombard next moved to Warner Brothers for one film because Jack Warner had recently offered Bette Davis, Errol Flynn, and Olivia de Havilland to David O. Selznick in return for twenty-five percent of *GWTW*'s profits. Davis had nixed this deal because she wasn't fond of Flynn, and Lombard hoped to sneak into the transaction at the last minute.

Warner had Carole in mind for another Flynn film then in the planning stage, *Four's a Crowd,* but when she signed her Warners contract, Jack Warner decided to put her to immediate use. He figured that screwball had to be easy since it was so prevalent, and ne ordered a script churned out in a matter of weeks. Charles Boyer, who had recently made the excellent *Tovarich* at Warners, read this new script and quickly turned it down.

It was a bad omen for Carole, who subsequently found the making of her one and only Warner Brothers film, *Fools for Scandal,* a dichotomous experience. She loved the studio and the people who worked there. But this particular production stank, and she well knew it. Director Mervyn LeRoy pretty much placed Lombard on a sound stage with humorless Belgian leading man Fernand Gravet and said, "Okay, be funny." *What?* She bit the bullet through a ghastly two months of filming and hoped against hope that the force of her comic personality would overshadow the weaknesses of the script. No wonder this studio didn't make screwball comedies; this studio had no sense of humor.

What a disaster. *Fools for Scandal* was released to reviewers who acted like ravenous canines and tore it to shreds. *Photoplay,* which liked almost everything that crossed its sights, said with a sneer that *Fools for Scandal* "probably will break the back of that slapstick camel Carole Lombard's been riding so long," while *Motion Picture* said it wasted her talent, the New York *Times* called it "ponderous," and a bewildered *Time* writer summed up the film best. It was, he said, "unearthly."

The people who knew her could tell she was shellshocked from the explosion of her Warner Brothers bomb. She grew so depressed that she stopped giving interviews. So depressed that she spent her evenings at home listening to Gable grouse about his number one problem, *Gone With the Wind,* a subject she now couldn't even bring herself to

mention. Her moroseness increased when Gable signed to
play the role of Rhett Butler on August 25, 1938.

In this mood, itching for a change away from "that
slapstick camel," Carole made her second Selznick feature,
the drama *Made for Each Other* with James Stewart. During
this second stay at Selznick's Culver City lot, Carole
took full advantage of the genius of Selznick publicity
whiz Russell Birdwell.

Birdwell was responsible for hoopla surrounding the
legendary Lombard tax return of 1937, wherein she earned
almost a half a million dollars and paid all but twenty
grand in taxes. Carole happened to mention that she didn't
mind being milked nearly dry by the government in exchange
for the opportunity to live in the greatest country in the
world. "Taxes go to build schools," said Carole, "to
maintain the public utilities we all use, so why not?"
(See source no. 087 and Chapter 4). Birdwell got wind of
this and fashioned from it a goldmine of favorable
publicity that earned Lombard applause from F. D. R. on
down.

Then there was the bronze tablet that remains affixed
to the house in Fort Wayne, Indiana in which Carole was
born in 1908. The inscription reads: "In this house, on
October 6, 1908, was born Jane Alice Peters, daughter of
Frederick C. and Elizabeth Knight Peters. She took the
professional name of Carole Lombard and became one of the
most important figures in the motion picture industry."
The tablet was unveiled in a splashy ceremony on New
Year's Day, 1938, with Carole begging off the crowds and
long trip but gleefully relishing newspaper accounts of
the festivities.

The high-water mark of all these schemes and all this
acclaim occurred in the autumn of 1938 when Carole graced
the cover of *Life* Magazine's October 17 issue. The
accompanying article, *A Loud Cheer for the Screwball Girl*,
contained over twenty photographs plus a great deal of
enlightening text. *Life* writer Noel F. Busch hit a bull's-
eye with his description of Lombard's renowned nervous
energy: "She gets up too early, plays tennis too hard,
wastes time and feeling on trifles and drinks Coca-Colas
the way Samuel Johnson used to drink tea. She is a scrib-
bler on telephone pads, inhibited nail-nibbler, toe scuf-
fler, pillow-grabber, head-and-elbow scratcher and chain
cigarette smoker. When Carole Lombard talks, her conversation, often brilliant, is punctuated by screeches,
laughs, growls, gesticulations, and the expletives of a
sailor's parrot." (See source no. 062).

As Carole's face stared out from the cover of *Life* at
newsstands across America, the Screwball Girl found herself confronting the unpleasant task of replacing Madalynne Fields as her secretary. Fieldsie was marrying director Walter Lang, and as a replacement Carole settled on
Jean Garceau, who had worked for the Myron Selznick Talent
Agency. Dubbed "Jeannie" by Carole, Garceau and Lombard
began a frantic hunt in the San Fernando Valley for a farm

suitable for a newly married couple--which Carole figured she and Clark would one day be.

After a long and unproductive search, Gable persuaded director Raoul Walsh (after years of trying) to part with his twenty acre weekend retreat in the San Fernando Valley, complete with a nine room farmhouse, three car garage, workshop, and other outbuildings. It was a place that would soon make the transition from reality to fable; the perfect home for the most perfect couple America had to offer.

The intention of Gable and Lombard was to eventually marry and settle here, but before this could happen, *Photoplay* Magazine ran an article by Kirtley Baskette entitled *Hollywood's Unmarried Husbands and Wives.* "*Just friends* to the world at large," read the teaser, "yet nowhere has domesticity taken on so unique a character as in this unconventional fold." (See source no. 050). The article itself detailed the exploits of chummy couples like George Raft and Virginia Pine, Robert Taylor and Barbara Stanwyck, Charlie Chaplin and Paulette Goddard, and yes, Lombard and Gable. In conservative America, this piece caused no small scandal and Baskette, who had previously received Lombard's full cooperation on stories, now entered her personal purgatory, from which there was no reprieve.

Both Carole and Clark fumed over the piece, yet a couple of years later, Lombard would have to admit that it had served as a catalyst for the divorce of Gable from his estranged wife, Ria Langham.

Undaunted by public criticism, in January, 1939 Carole signed a radio deal for a Sunday evening program to be called *The Circle*, featuring an all-star cast of articulate performers expounding on current issues, various philosophies of life and death, and opinions on film, music, and literature. Carole earned five thousand a week for this unorthodox venture, as did Ronald Colman. Also in the original cast were Cary Grant and Groucho and Chico Marx. (See also page 79).

It was a clever idea, but an idea whose time had not yet come. Imagine how America felt when it tuned in *The Circle* on Sunday evening, January 22, 1939 expecting to be entertained, and instead heard Carole Lombard making the following unconventional speech to Cary Grant and the other members of the panel: "You can mark my words, Cary Grant, some day we'll have a woman president."

She then launched into a lengthy commentary on the troubled world situation (civil war in Spain, Hitler's annexation of whole countries, Great Britain's acts of appeasement) and speculated on the likely state of things, if only women could be in charge: "If women ran this world it would be a better world. It wouldn't be such a sorry mess of a world. It wouldn't be the kind of a world that bombs kids in the streets and taxes their parents to pay for the bombs...It would be a cleaner place, a saner place, a finer place because...women are realists. They wouldn't permit war because everybody knows nobody can win a war.   They wouldn't permit slums and filth and disease and poverty because those things cost everybody money.   Do you know what causes war and poverty? All right, I'll tell you. Male stupidity, male sentiment and male greed."

She wholeheartedly believed in the concept of *The Circle*; its weekly execution, however, left much to be desired.   Scripts were weak and payments ran late, and within a month, Carole became the show's first casualty. Other stars appeared, with Groucho Marx soon taking over, but since the entire project lacked direction, and since Groucho wasn't a universally accepted personality, *The Circle* sank behind the horizon in July, 1939.

With this new failure added to a growing list, the perpetual motion machine that was Carole Lombard suddenly ran low on energy.   It was a sad sight to behold; she seemed content to call herself Clark Gable's "unmarried wife" and nothing more.   The only place she showed up in public was at Gilmore Field on Beverly Boulevard, where she and Clark owned season tickets to watch the Hollywood Stars of the Pacific Coast League play baseball.   Other- wise, she enjoyed no social life at all.

Then rumors began to fly, a month after *Gone With the Wind* began filming, that Lombard and Gable would finally marry. Reporters staked out Lombard's St. Cloud Road home, putting a lid on Clark and Carole's nightly rendezvous. No self-respecting columnist would dare miss the elopement of Hollywood's royal couple.

At dawn on Wednesday, March 29, 1939, during a short Gable hiatus from *GWTW*, he and Carole conducted a daring top-secret elopement to Kingman, Arizona, and were mar- ried.

The now subdued, contented and, some said, grown up Carole Lombard signed a new four-picture contract with RKO Studios at a rate of $150,000 per film while at the same time entertaining long-range plans to retire from the screen so she could devote herself to Clark and family life.

Her first project at RKO was *Memory of Love*, retitled *In Name Only*, with old friends Cary Grant and Kay Francis. Later, *In Name Only* would appear to a lukewarm reception, paling as it did to such exhilarating entertainments as *Dodge City* and *Drums Along the Mohawk*.

Smarting again, the newlywed Carole was largely alone since Gable had yet to complete filming of *Gone With the Wind,* and she sought distraction by spending nearly every waking hour redecorating the Encino ranch at 4525 Petit Avenue.   It was as close as Carole would ever get to her idea of a dream house, and her idea of home.

In July, after *GWTW* had finally wrapped, the Gables moved to Encino--Clark from his rented home in North Hollywood, Carole from her self-styled farm in Bel Air. They then spent a glorious August and September that would prove the most heavenly period in the profane angel's all

*Lombard and Gable leave their chartered DC-3 in Atlanta, December, 1939.
(Photo from the collection of Susan Marie Rice.)*

David O. Selznick, Vivien Leigh, Victor Fleming, Carole Lombard, and Clark Gable, 1939.

too short life. She and Clark went riding, shot skeet and
target, tried farming, chose servants, and watched sunsets
from the hill above their back door.
     Then in October, 1939, just before she was supposed
to begin work on the film *Vigil in the Night,* Lombard
suddenly took ill.   For the record, she supposedly under-
went an appendectomy, although Gable biographer Lyn Tornabene suggests a different malady: "Three days before she
was to start work, she was in Cedars of Lebanon hospital
with a disease highly contagious in Hollywood: appendici-
tis. She reportedly had an appendectomy and was home in a
few days, at work within three weeks. Maybe it was. Maybe she did. Surely some of the reported appendectomies in
filmland involved somebody's appendix being removed, but
some friends claim Carole had a miscarriage.   Maybe she
did." (See source no. 039).
     If Carole did indeed suffer a miscarriage, it would
be her one and only brush with pregnancy and with this in
mind, her later obsession with having children is much
more understandable. Whatever the malady, her crash course
in hospital care came in handy for *Vigil in the Night,* the
stark doctor-nurse film she finally started two weeks after being released from Cedars of Lebanon.
     Upon its completion, Carole accompanied Clark to
Atlanta, Georgia for *GWTW*'s tumultuous premiere, and
virtually babysat Hollywood's King through an ordeal he
detested. Most painful to her was Clark's feud with David
O. Selznick, which effectively voided Carole's remaining
picture commitment to Selznick International. (See source
no. 001).
     When she returned from Atlanta, she was contacted by
Orson Welles about appearing in a film version of the
Nicholas Blake novel *Smiler with a Knife*, and she sensed
it was the kind of role she had wanted a year earlier,
after *Fools for Scandal.*   Unfortunately, Welles admitted
that RKO didn't have the money to bankroll him right away,
and *Smiler* was ultimately discarded.
     Carole found herself on hiatus again and began
showing up at MGM in surprise inspections of her husband's
dressing room, looking for signs of Gable's *Boom Town* co-
star, Hedy Lamarr, supposedly a Gable conquest.   Carole
took such talk seriously because she and Clark were still
trying to become parents, something they by now treated
with great solemnity in private, although publicly she
joked about it with everybody. "He's the worst lay I ever
had in all my life," Groucho Marx reported Lombard as once
saying about Gable. Did she mean it? Lyn Tornabene keen-
ly observed: "Chances are...that if Gable weren't Gable at
anything, Carole—a self-appointed guardian of her husband's image—would be the last person in the world to say
so. (See source no. 039).
     At this late date, with their first anniversary just
passed, with a new ranch and with the fact that she might
show up pregnant any day, she wasn't about to lose the
promiscuous Gable to the first gorgeous face that came

along. And Hedy Lamarr was plenty gorgeous. It was therefore a blessing when Carole's next film, *They Knew What
They Wanted,* began filming at RKO and she could go to work
every day, turning her mind off to everything but memori-
zing lines and hitting her marks.   This was her fourth
dramatic film in a row, which Carole maintained was a
coincidence. She told the Associated Press on Sept. 30,
1939 that these roles "just came my way and looked like
they had guts. If it's a good part in a good story, that's
all that counts."
     Her high hopes regarding this new project faded
quickly in what turned out to be an unhappy production
marked by the very eccentric Charles Laughton taking
liberties with his young director, Garson Kanin, and his
young co-star. He went on tantrums, often claimed he
couldn't *feel* the part, and generally treated Lombard like
a pestering bill collector instead of a veteran colleague.
(See source no. 021).
     Conversely, she delighted in working with photograph-
er Harry Stradling, who in turn said of Lombard: "She
knows as much about the tricks of the trade as I do!   In
close-up work, I wanted to cover her scar simply by focus-
ing the lights on her face so that it would seem to blend
with her cheek.   She told me a diffusing glass in my lens
would do the same job better.   And she was right!" (See
source no. 027).
     The experience of making *They Knew What They Wanted,*
intense as it was, rekindled her desire for the motion
picture business to such an extent that while she and
Clark now spent another carefree, party-filled summer at
the ranch, Lombard ended up making statements to the effect that filmmaking was in her blood, and she didn't honestly believe she could permanently give it up.
     In late summer, 1940, Carole received a script from
RKO entitled *Mr. and Mrs. Smith,* a pleasant, light little
story that, she decided, would mark her return to the
genre of comedy.   The world needed a few laughs these
days, what with the worsening European situation.
     Before RKO could come up with a freelance director to
handle *Mr. and Mrs. Smith,* Lombard set about convincing
Alfred Hitchcock,   fresh from an impressive career in
Great Britain, to do the job. With her considerable
clout, it wasn't tough to get RKO to borrow Hitchcock from
David Selznick for a two picture stint there (*Suspicion*
would be his second RKO film made under the terms of this
contract).   The Englishman agreed to take on *Mr. and Mrs.
Smith* strictly as a favor to Lombard; it clearly wasn't a
Hitchcock brand of project. (See source no. 040).
     As 1940 gave way to 1941, the Gables journeyed east
to Johns Hopkins Medical Center in Baltimore for tests to
determine why they couldn't have children.   They then
visited the Roosevelts in the White House, an event that
awed the Democrat in Lombard.
     When they returned to Hollywood, they received the
test results: everything normal. Except that she *couldn't*

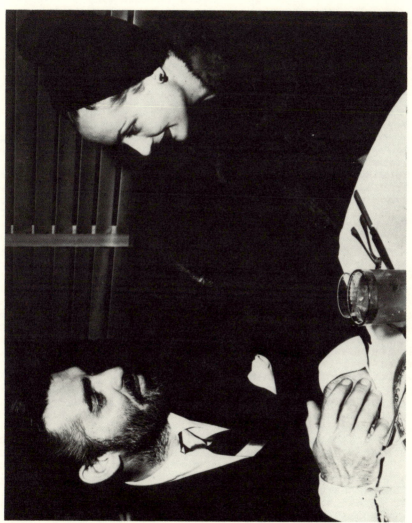

Lombard and Gable in 1940; Carole's cheek and eye scars are plainly visible. (Photo from the collection of Susan Marie Rice.)

get pregnant. Thus storm clouds gathered over the story-book, flower-laden Encino ranch, and neither Lombard nor Gable could have had the slightest inkling that their best times were now behind them. The situation intensified when Gable started working with sexy young Lana Turner, causing Lombard's jealous streak to flare. Rumors of a breakup suddenly flew like so much ragweed on a windy day, although Turner consistently denied that any physical contact between the two ever took place. "There was a dear loving for him," Lana said, "but never an affair. No way." (See source no. 041).

As Clark worked, Carole remained unhappily inactive for several months until she finally found a script to her liking. In October she went back to work in United Artists' black comedy *To Be or Not to Be,* produced and directed by old friend Ernst Lubitsch. The story was timely, centering on European life under the ruling Nazis; what better way to alert America to the dangers of Nazi Germany, Carole reasoned, than through this sugar-coated but vitally important dose of medicine?

Sensing her zeal, Lubitsch allowed Carole to act as the unofficial producer of the film, and she responded by casting minor roles, editing the script as needed, and generally engaging in a cathartic, long dreamed-of stint behind the camera, as well as in front of it.

The leading man of *To Be or Not to Be* was Jack Benny, a likeable and talented veteran of the radio wars, but still a novice in motion pictures. Benny would ask co-star Robert Stack after a scene, "Does it work? Is it funny?" Stack would throw up his hands. "Jack, this is only my fourth picture. Why are you asking me? This is *your* racket, not mine." (From Robert Stack interview, 18 March 1986). Carole was in her glory, playing mother hen to the insecure likes of Stack and Benny, finding new and creative uses for her overflowing energy. All in all, it was her most enjoyable film experience in years.

Until Sunday, December 7, that is.

Attacked by who? The Japs? Where? Pearl Harbor-- where the hell is that? War? Oh my God, no. Everybody figured the Nazis would start it, not their Axis ally, the Japanese.

To grasp the geopolitical situation of 1941 is key to understanding the Carole Lombard of that same period, a super-patriot, a pragmatist who understood the score, who didn't want to see anybody die if it could be avoided. But blood had been spilled, Americans had been bushwacked, a wrong had been done to *us,* and the two hours of hell that was Pearl Harbor instantly polarized America, necessarily so, into a nation of holy crusaders seeking revenge.

The next day, Roosevelt gave his Day of Infamy speech, and Carole and Clark wrote to the President, offering their services in any way, shape, or form that might be helpful. A letter came back from the White House telling them to continue with their usual schedules, that the entertainment industry was vital to a disrupted nation.

Gable accepted this idea hands down, with great relief. He *was* forty years old, slowing down, and he *was* married. None of which curbed his wife's disappointment.

It was at about this time that columnist Adela Rogers St. Johns stopped at the ranch for a visit and heard Carole's vague query, "Do you believe in God?" The question stuck with St. Johns, haunted her, and formed an integral part of an article for *Liberty* Magazine. (See source no. 122).

Christmas, usually Carole's favorite, most animated time of year, came and went quietly. Gable gave his wife diamond and ruby jewelry, as he always did, but there was little to celebrate at Christmas, 1941.

By now, Gable had been appointed chairman of the Screen Actors division of the Hollywood Victory Committee, and the White House strongly advised that he make a few appearances in Ohio, his home state, to sell war bonds. But the King didn't like attention focused on himself, even after all those years in the limelight. No, he told the government, a bond-selling tour wouldn't do at all.

In desperation, with Carole needling Clark to first sell bonds in Ohio, then join the army, Clark responded to the effect that, "You go sell bonds. *You go!"*

This suited Carole just fine.

On January 12, 1942, Lombard, her mother, Bessie Peters, and MGM publicity man Otto Winkler boarded a train and headed east for a bond rally in Indianapolis. They stopped in Salt Lake City and Ogden, Utah, and arrived in Chicago on January 14.

January 15 in Indianapolis was cold and windy--the dead of winter in North America. Carole toured the city at the center of a cyclone of activity. In front of the Indiana State House she ended her speech with, "Let's give a rousing cheer that'll be heard in Berlin and Tokyo!" (See source no. 013). Then, in the capitol rotunda, the bond sale commenced with a goal of a half million dollars. Lombard gave an autograph with every bond purchased, and kept urging on the crowd until more than two million dollars had been collected--four times the projection.

With the motorcade, the crowds, the reporters, the popping flashbulbs, with the high bond sale and the climactic Cadle Tabernacle rally that drew twelve thousand people, and with Carole leading the assembled crowd in a stirring rendition of the National Anthem as she raised her arms above her head in a V for Victory, Lombard's star ascended to its highest point. This was, in all probability, the most exciting day of her life.

Hours later, at the Indianapolis Municipal Airport, Carole fully intented to race home to the ranch by air, owing to a mixture of fatigue and jealousy at Gable's rumored fling with young Lana Turner, with whom he was about to begin the MGM film *Somewhere I'll Find You*. Otto Winkler was also exhausted and near tears as he pleaded

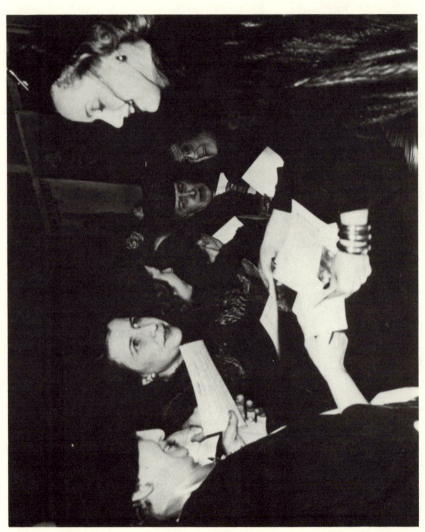

Carole Lombard selling war bonds in Indianapolis on the day before her death, January 15, 1942.

with Carole to stick   to the prearranged schedule and take the   train back home.   The government specifically wanted her   on a train to avoid mishaps and even   sabotage;   Otto had been instructed by everybody to see that   Carole   obey this   order.   But how did one *order* Carole Lombard to   do anything?

The best she would do was flip for it.   Heads,   train, tails plane.   It came up tails and she *thought* that would be that.   Still Otto griped,   as did Carole's mother. Numerologist Bessie already possessed a terrible fear   of flying.   On top of that,   the signs were all   bad.   She sensed trouble.

Three was a hard luck number.   They were flying a DC-3.   Their   plane   would   be   Flight *3* from   New   York   to Burbank.   Carole was *thirty-three* years and *three*   months old.   And there were *three* people in their party.

Bessie mustered her strength,   grabbed her daughter's arm,   and exclaimed within earshot of reporters,   "Carole, we must not take that plane!"   (From   The New York *Times*, 18 January 1942).

As if rushing toward her destiny, Carole would not be dissuaded.   Myron Davis,   the *Life* Magazine photographer who had covered the rally,   engaged Lombard in   conversation,   unwittingly   stumbling   into the   argument   between Carole   and her mother.   Carole told Davis   she   couldn't face   three days on the "choo-choo train," and that in the time it would take to spend the night in   a   hotel,   then catch   the   train,   she   could nearly be home on   a   DC-3. Davis   commented   that she looked tired.   She   waved   her hand.   "When I get home,   I'll flop in bed and sleep   for twelve hours."   (See source no. 066).

With Bessie and Otto still grousing,   at 4 a.m.   they boarded   the   TWA Douglas Sky Club that had just flown   in from LaGuardia.   The trip to St.   Louis took four   hours. They   landed at 8 a.m.   to refuel and pick up   passengers. Subsequent stops occurred in Kansas City,   Wichita,   Albu-querque, and finally Las Vegas.

At   7:07,   the refueled plane took off from Las Vegas and fifteen minutes later crashed   into Double-Up Peak   in the   Sierra   Nevada   Mountains   southwest   of   Las   Vegas. Lombard,   her mother,   and Otto Winkler all perished nearly instantly,   fulfilling   Carole's   earlier feeling that she would die young.

It took two days to bring the fragmented bodies   down the   mountain.   A   grief-stricken Gable   accompanied   the three   sets   of remains back to Los Angeles by   train   for burial at Forest Lawn.

In   Hollywood,   the news of her death hit   hard,   and nobody could quite believe that the high octane Screwball Girl   had left them.   When reporters asked for   comments, they   were   met   with   profound   silence.   Fieldsie   had collapsed in grief.   William Powell leaned on Diana Lewis, his wife of two years, for support.   "There is nothing one can say,"   Robert Taylor observed.   "It is too   terrible." (From The New York *Times*, 19 January 1942).   Now faced

with a very real war that could move in and snatch one of
its own--its best and brightest--with devastating ease,
Hollywood seemed to grow up overnight.

A notably somber Errol Flynn said, "Carole Lombard's
death means that something of gaiety and of beauty has
been taken from the world at a time such things are needed
most." (From The New York Times, 19 January 1942).

At noon on Monday, January 19, taps sounded in Hollywood, and all employees of all studios stood in silent
meditation. Indiana Senator Raymond E. Willis read a
tribute in Congress.   President Roosevelt sent a telegram
to Gable that read: "Mrs. Roosevelt and I are deeply dis-
tressed. Carole was our friend, our guest in happier
days. She brought great joy to all who knew her and to
millions who knew her only as a great artist. She gave
unselfishly of time and talent to serve her government in
peace and in war. She loved her country. She is and always will be a star, one we shall never forget nor cease
to be grateful to." (See source no. 004).

The funeral, a simple affair as specified in
Lombard's will, was held for both Carole and Bessie at 4
p.m. on Wednesday at Forest Lawn's Church of the Reces-
sional before interment in the Sanctity of Trust hallway
of the Great Mausoleum, resting place of both Russ Columbo
and Jean Harlow.

In the ensuing eighteen years, Gable would blame
himself for his wife's death and never grasp the inevita-
bility of it.   Carole had cheerfully accepted his offer
to go sell bonds; he hadn't forced her. After this trip
would have come another and another, followed by entertaining the troops overseas and heaven only knew what
else. She was born for legend, born to expend great
bursts of energy in a frantic, short lifetime.

Within months of the plane crash, Gable, the guy who
had once thought himself too old to fight in a war, suddenly signed up with the Air Force. He went in as a private, carried a death wish with him throughout World War
II, flew combat missions over Germany while serving as a
gunner, and emerged two years later a major. He went on
to live a full life that included two more marriages, but
through all those eighteen years, Carole haunted him as
she haunted all those who knew her. She simply couldn't
be replaced. Not as a wife, a movie star, a socialite, a
comedienne, or a friend.

She was the first noted American to die in World War
II and since her death held such purpose, the legend was
fueled and the sorrow grew oppressive. She was an actress
who made a few memorable films, two or three of which are
now called "classics," yet the bulk of her work is routine
because she discovered her own true talents relatively
late in her career.

At the time of Jean Harlow's death in 1937, Lombard
had just been nominated for an Academy Award for My Man
Godfrey and lost to Luise Rainer. Caught in a philosophi-
cal moment, Carole had death on her mind and told reporter

William French how she would like to be remembered after she was gone. "Jean had it," said Carole, "a humanness that makes your passing leave a void no one can ever quite fill. If I had that, the other fellow could have the Oscars." (See source no. 081). Clearly, she too had *it*. The late-blooming actress, and the sympathetic friend of the underdog, left a void that no one has ever come close to filling. Luckily for us all, her legacy also includes the memory of a life so truly well-lived that Hollywood still quakes from the sheer force of her will.

2.   A Lombard Chronology

1908   Born Jane Alice Peters in Fort Wayne, Indiana on
        October 6.   Parents Frederick Peters and Eliza-
        beth Knight Peters.

1914   Moves to Los Angeles with mother and two broth-
        ers after parents separate.

1921   Spotted by Allan Dwan and cast in *A Perfect
        Crime*.

1924   Voted May Queen of Fairfax High and offered
        screen by Charlie Chaplin as a result.

        Signs Fox Studios contract on sixteenth birthday
        and chooses stage name Carol Lombard.

1925   Suffers facial injuries in automobile accident.
        Eighteen month layoff ensues.

1927   Signs contract with Mack Sennett Comedies.

1928   Signs contract with Pathe Studios.

1930   Signs seven year contract with Paramount.

        Adds *e* to Carol after noticing this spelling
        as a mistake by the ad department.

1931   Marries William Powell after a six month court-
        ship.

        Signs with the Myron Selznick Talent Agency.

1933   Divorces Powell amicably; begins serious rela-
        tionship with singer Russ Columbo.

1934   Cast in *Twentieth Century* opposite John Barry-
        more, her first noteworthy success.

Columbo dies in shooting accident several months before they are to be married.

1935   Father dies in Ann Arbor, Michigan following brain surgery.

1936   Begins relationship with Clark Gable.

Makes *My Man Godfrey* and scores biggest success to date, including Academy Award nomination.

Legally changes name to Carole Lombard, adopting it for business use.

1937   Becomes the highest-paid actress in Hollywood during the last year of her Paramount contract.

Signs three year contract with Selznick International Studios. Makes *Nothing Sacred* for that studio, her first Technicolor feature, and a critical success.

1939   Signs contract to appear in radio talk show called *The Circle* but withdraws after one month.

Marries Clark Gable in Arizona. Buys twenty acre ranch with Gable in Encino, California.

1940   Suffers appendectomy--or miscarriage.

Travels with Gable to Washington for fertility tests; visits President Roosevelt in the White House.

1941   Completes last film, *To Be or Not to Be,* two weeks after the bombing of Pearl Harbor.

1942   Killed along with mother, MGM publicity man Otto Winkler, and nineteen others in Nevada plane crash on January 16 after successful war bond tour to Indianapolis.

3. Film and Radio Appearances

A Perfect Crime (1921)
Dwan Associates.

Director and Writer:	Allan Dwan
Photographer:	Lyman Broening
Original Story:	Carl Clausen
Running time:	5 reels

Cast

Wally Griggs	Monte Blue
Mary Oliver	Jacqueline Logan
"Big Bill" Thaine	Stanton Heck
President Halliday	Hardee Kirkland
Grigg's sister	Jane Peters

Summary: Jane Peters' inauguration into the film world encompassed three scenes portraying the young sister of a Walter Mitty-type hero. This is now considered a lost film, with only production stills remaining.

Dick Turpin (1925)
Fox.

Director:	John G. Blystone
Writers:	Charles Kenyon and Charles Darnton
Running time:	72 minutes

Cast

Dick Turpin	Tom Mix
Lord Churlton	Philo McCullough
Squire Crabtree	James Marcus
Sally	Lucile Hutton
Tom King	Alan Hale

Summary: Jane Peters' first work at Fox under the   name
Carol Lombard involved one scene with Mix,   plus a   group
scene.   Only the group shot remained in the final print.

Gold and the Girl (1925)
Fox.
Director: Edmund Mortimer
Writer: John Stone
Running time: 53 minutes

Cast: Buck Jones, Elinor Fair,   Bruce Gordon,   Lucien
Littlefield, Claude Peyton, Carol Lombard, Alphonz Ethier.

Summary: A standard western containing a brief walk-on by
Lombard, although she wasn't billed.

Marriage in Transit (1925)
Fox.
Director: Roy William Neill
Story: Grace Livingston Hill
Adaptation: Dorothy Yost
Running time: 53 minutes

Cast

Holden/Cyril Gordon	Edmund Lowe
Celia Hathaway	Carol Lombard
Haynes	Adolph Milar
Burnham	Frank Beal
Aide	Harvey Clarke
Valet	Fred Walton

Summary: So impressed was Fox Studios head Winfield
Sheehan with his sixteen year old discovery Lombard that
he gambled and thrust her into the second lead role in
this improbable story of a secret agent infiltrating a
gang   of conspirators.   No known print exists, but the
film received good reviews, as did the inexperienced
Lombard.

Hearts and Spurs (1925)
Fox.
Director: W. S. Van Dyke
Screenplay: John Stone
Original Story: Jackson Gregory
Photography: Allen Davey
Running time: 52 minutes

Cast

Hal Emory	Charles (Buck) Jones
Sybil Estabrook	Carol Lombard

Victor Dufresne	William Davidson
Oscar Estabrook	Freeman Wood
Celeste	Jean Lamott
Sid Thomas	J. Gordon Russell

Summary: Lombard portrays the hero's love interest   in this typically plotted early western directed by   "Woody" Van Dyke,   who would later gain considerable notoriety at MGM.

Durand of the Badlands (1925)
Fox.

Director:	Lynn Reynolds
Screenplay:	Lynn Reynolds
Original story:	Maibelle Heikes Justice
Running Time:	62 minutes

Cast

Dick Durand	Charles (Buck) Jones
Molly Gore	Marion Nixon
Clem Allison	Malcolm Waite
Pete Garson	Fred De Silva
Kingdom Come Knapp	Luke Cosgrove
John Boyd	George Lessley
Jimmie	Buck Black
Clara Belle Seesel	Ann Johnson
Joe Gore	James Corrigan
Ellen Boyd	Carol Lombard

Summary: Fox's early disillusionment with Lombard is evidenced by the fact that she was tenth-billed in another Jones western,   appearing as a damsel in distress rescued by the hero. The film was released shortly after her automobile accident.

The Road to Glory (1926)
Fox.

Director:	Howard Hawks
Screenplay:	L. G. Rigby
Original Story:	Howard Hawks
Photography:	Joseph August
Running time:	93 minutes

Cast

Judith Allen	May McAvoy
David Hale	Leslie Fenton
James Allen	Ford Sterling
Del Cole	Rockliffe Fellowes

Summary: Hawks' first film as director had just begun production when Lombard, who had been cast in a   minor role, received severe facial injuries in the auto accident. She was replaced in the film, although she appears in two scenes.

The Fighting Eagle (1927)
Pathe.

Director:	Donald Crisp
Screenplay:	Douglas Doty
Titles	John Kraft
Story:	Sir Arthur Conan Doyle
Running time:	85 minutes

Cast

Etienne Gerard	Rod La Rocque
Countess de Launay	Phyllis Haver
Tallyrand	Sam de Grasse
Napoleon Bonapart	Max Barwyn
Josephine	Julia Faye

Summary: Of this film, Lombard biographer Larry Swindell states: "Rod La Rocque insisted that Carole Lombard had played a small part in this costume film produced by Cecil B. DeMille's unit. Mitchell Leisen, the art director, doubted Carole's participation, but Donald Crisp verified that he had once directed Carole Lombard in a silent feature, so presumably, this was it." (See source no. 036).

Smith's Pony (1927)
Sennett-Pathe.

Director:	Alf Goulding
Running time:	2 reels

Cast: Raymond McKee, Ruth Hiatt, Mary Ann Jackson, Carol, Lombard, Billy Gilbert.

Summary: Carol's first Mack Sennett short is typically entertaining, involving a husband, wife, and young son on a passenger ship, with Lombard the young ingenue who, the wife incorrectly suspects, is having an affair with the husband. Lombard had good reason to feel optimistic about her future with Sennett after her debut in this film.

A Gold Digger of Weepah (1927)
Sennett-Pathe.

Director:	Harry Edwards
Running time:	2 reels

Cast: Billy Bevan, Madeline Hurlock, Vernon Dent, Carol Lombard.

Summary: Lombard's second Sennett short introduced her to such comedic veterans as Bevan and Dent; the later would go on to dozens of appearances in Three Stooges shorts.

The Girl from Everywhere (1927)
Sennett-Pathe.
Director: Edward Cline
Screenplay: Harry McCoy, Vernon Smith
Running time: 2 reels

Cast: Daphne Pollard, Dot Farley, Mack Swain, Carol Lombard, Irving Bacon, Madalynne Fields.

Summary: This short contained the best of the Sennett company—Pollard and Swain—and afforded Lombard her first opportunity to work with Madalynne Fields.

Run, Girl, Run (1928)
Sennett-Pathe.
Director: Alf Goulding
Screenplay: Harry McCoy, James Tynan
Film Editor: William Hornbeck
Running time: 2 reels

Cast: Daphne Pollard, Carol Lombard, Irving Bacon, Dot Farley, Madalynne Fields.

Summary: After appearing as a "stock player" in her first three Sennett shorts, Carol played the featured role of the girl's school's star athlete.   Never modest about her state of undress on-screen, she stripped down to lingerie in a scene with Pollard, and her abilities as a runner are evident throughout. Key scenes were shot in Technicolor.

The Beach Club (1928)
Sennett-Pathe.
Director: Harry Edwards
Story: Jefferson Moffitt,
                                     Harry McCoy
Running time: 2 reels

Cast: Billy Bevan, Madeline Hurlock, Carol Lombard, Vernon Dent.

Summary: No information available.

The Best Man (1928)
Sennett-Pathe.
Director: Harry Edwards
Supervision: John A. Waldron
Running time: 2 reels

Cast: Billy Bevan, Alma Bennett, Vernon Dent, Carol Lombard, Andy Clyde, Bill Searley.

Summary: No information available.

The Swim Princess (1928)
Sennett-Pathe.

Director:	Alf Goulding
Supervision:	John Waldron
Screenplay:	James Tynan, Frank Capra
Film Editor:	William Hornbeck
Running time:	2 reels

Cast: Daphne Pollard, Andy Clyde, Carol Lombard, Cissie Fitzgerald.

Summary: Lombard is again the centerpiece, this time as the star swimmer. Technicolor sequences are included, with the script co-written by Frank Capra.

The Bicycle Flirt (1928)
Sennett-Pathe.

Director:	Harry Edwards
Screenplay:	Vernon Smith, Harry McCoy
Running time:	2 reels

Cast: Billy Bevan, Vernon Dent, Carol Lombard.

Summary: Lombard plays the girl seduced by the title character.

Half a Bride (1928)
Paramount.

Director:	Gregory LaCava
Story:	Doris Anderson, Percy Heath
Titles:	Julian Johnson
Running time:	70 minutes

Cast: Esther Ralston, Gary Cooper, William Worthington, Freeman Wood, Mary Doran, Guy Oliver, Ray Gallagher.

Summary: A lost film containing a Lombard bit part. Directed by LaCava, whose association with Carol would prove to be quite profitable.

The Divine Sinner (1928)
Rayart/Trem Carr.

Director:	Scott Pembroke
Screenplay:	Robert Anthony Dillon
Photography:	Hap Depew

Film Editor:	J. E. Harrington
Running time:	60 minutes

Cast

Lillia Ludwig	Vera Reynolds
Minister of Police	Nigel De Brulier
Johann Ludwig	Bernard Seigel
Prince Josef Miguel	Ernest Hilliard
Lugue Bernstorff	John Peters
Millie Claudert	Carol Lombard
Ambassador D'Ray	Harry Northrup

Summary: This low-budget film seems lost to antiquity, with no known prints extant. The story involves the adventures of Reynolds as Lillia in Paris, including a convoluted royal conspiracy. Lombard is given little to do.

Girl From Nowhere (1928)
Sennett-Pathe.

Director:	Harry Edwards
Story:	Ewart Anderson,
	Jefferson Moffitt
Running time:	2 reels

Cast: Daphne Pollard, Dot Farley, Mack Swain, Sterling Holloway, Madalynne Fields, Carol Lombard.

Summary: Lombard portrays, logically enough, a motion picture performer in a typical Sennett short.

His Unlucky Night (1928)
Sennett-Pathe.

Director:	Harry Edwards
Supervisor:	John A. Waldron
Story:	Vernon Smith, Nick Barrows
Film Editor:	William Hornbeck
Running time:	2 reels

Cast: Billy Bevan, Vernon Dent, Carol Lombard.

Summary: No information available.

Power (1928)
Pathe.

Producer:	Ralph Block
Director:	Howard Higgin
Story:	Tay Garnett
Photography:	Peverell Marley
Titles:	John Kraft
Running time:	65 minutes

Cast

Quirt	William Boyd
Flagg	Alan Hale
Lorraine La Rue	Jacqueline Logan
The Menace	Jerry Drew
A Dame	Joan Bennett
Another Dame	Carol Lombard
Still Another Dame	Pauline Curley

Summary: Having signed with Pathe, Lombard was first given a minor, unnamed role here, in a strongly cast story of two boisterous skirt-chasers.

The Campus Vamp (1928)
Sennett-Pathe.
Director: Alf Goulding
Story: Jefferson Moffitt,
                                 Earle Rodney
Running time: 2 reels

Cast: Daphne Pollard, Jefferson Moffitt, Earle Rodney, Carol Lombard.

Summary: Another beach comedy with the Bathing Beauties.

Me, Gangster (1928)
Fox.
Director: Raoul Walsh
Screenplay: Charles Francis Coe,
                                 Raoul Walsh
Photographer: Arthur Edeson
Running time: 70 minutes

Cast

Mary Regan	June Collyer
Jimmy Williams	Don Terry
Russ Williams	Anders Randolf
Lizzie Williams	Stella Adams
Danny	Al Hill
Bill Lane, Boss	Burr McIntosh
Police Captain Dodds	Walter James
Factory Owner	Gustav von Seyffertitz
Sucker	Herbert Ashton
Philly Kidd	Harry Cattle
Joe Brown	Joe Brown
Dan the dude	Arthur Stone
Danish Looie	Nigel De Brulier
Blonde Rosie	Carol Lombard

Summary: Lombard portrays a floozy in this cops-and-robbers melodrama directed by the noted Walsh.

Show Folks (1928)
Pathe.

Director:	Paul L. Stein
Screenplay:	Jack Jungmeyer, George Dromgold
Story:	Phillip Dunning
Titles:	John Kraft
Photography:	Peverell Marley, Dave Abel
Art Director:	Mitchell Leisen
Running time:	70 minutes

Cast

Eddie	Eddie Quillan
Rita	Lina Basquette
Cleo	Carol Lombard
Owens	Robert Armstrong
McNary	Crawford Kent
Kitty	Bessie Barriscale

Summary: The story of two dancers; notable because of its musical score and ten minutes of dialogue as the sound era approached. Art Director Leisen would become one of Lombard's closest friends.

The Campus Carmen (1928)
Sennett-Pathe.

Director:	Alf Goulding
Screenplay:	Jefferson Moffitt, Earle Rodney
Running time:	2 reels

Cast: Carol Lombard, Sally Eilers, Vernon Dent, Carmelita Geraghty, Marry Kemp, Madalynne Fields.

Summary: Technicolor sections highlight a good Sennett short about an amateurish production of *Carmen* complete with a pantomime bull that attacks Daphne Pollard in hilarious fashion.

Ned McCobb's Daughter (1928)
Pathe.

Director:	William J. Cowen
Screenplay:	Marie Beulah Dix
Play:	Sidney Howard
Photography:	David Abel
Film Editor:	Ann Banchens
Art Director:	Edward Jewell
Production Manager:	John Rohefs
Titles:	John Kraft
Running time:	71 minutes

Carol Lombard in 1929.

Cast

Carrie McCobb	Irene Rich
Ned McCobb	Theodore Roberts
Babe Callahan	Robert Armstrong
George Callahan	George Baeraud
Butterworth	George Hearn
Jennie	Carol Lombard
Kelly	Louis Natheaux

Summary: A late silent film about bootletting and murder, in which Lombard has a secondary role as a waitress.

Matchmaking Mamas (1929)
Sennett-Pathe.

Director:	Harry Edwards
Supervision:	John A. Waldron
Story:	Jefferson Moffitt,
	Carl Harbaugh
Film Editor:	William Hornbeck
Running time:	2 reels

Cast: Johnny Burke, Matty Kemp, Sally Eilers, Carol Lombard.

Summary: Notable as Lombard's last silent film, and her last film for Mack Sennett.

High Voltage (1929)
Pathe.

Director:	Howard Higgins
Story:	Elliott Clawson
Screenplay:	James Gleason,
	Kenyon Nicholson
Photography:	John Mescall
Film Editor:	Doane Harrison
Running time:	57 minutes

Cast

The Boy	William Boyd
The Girl	Carol Lombard
The Detective	Owen Moore
The Banker	Phillips Smalley
The Driver	Billy Bevan
The Kid	Diane Ellis

Summary: Lombard portrays a prisoner on her way to jail in a melodrama set in the snowy Sierra Nevada.   This was her first all-talking picture, featuring performances by all that would have been better suited to a sub-par high school play.

Big News (1929)
Pathe.

Director:	Gregory LaCava
Screenplay:	Walter De Leon
Play:	George S. Brooks
Adaptation:	Jack Jungmeyer
Photography:	Arthur Miller
Dialogue:	Frank Reicher
Film Editor:	Doane Harrison
Running time:	75 minutes

Cast

Steve Banks	Robert Armstrong
Mrs. Banks	Carol Lombard
Reno	Sam Hardy
Patrolman Ryan	Tom Kennedy
Hansel	Louis Payne
O'Neil	Wade Boetler
Editor	Charles Sellon

Summary: A newspaper-game story that received good reviews, as did Lombard in the role of a reporter. The New York *Times* said, "Carol Lombard, as the female reporter, is a step above the ingenue film heroine and manages her part with sufficient restraint."

Dynamite (1929)
Pathe.

Director:	Cecil B. DeMille
Story, Screenplay:	Jeanie MacPherson
Assistant Director:	Mitchell Leisen
Additional dialogue:	John Lawson, Gladys Unger
Running time:	118 minutes

Cast

Roger Towne	Conrad Nagel
Cynthia Crothers	Kay Johnson
Hagon Derk	Charles Bickford
Marcia Towne	Julia Faye

Summary: Although Lombard was fired in mid-production, she is visible in the final print. Her role was recast, and she received no billing. Madalynne Fields played a small role in the film. DeMille would later host the Lux Radio Theatre, on which Lombard was a frequent guest. On her first appearance, he was forced to confront his earlier decision. "A few years ago I selected two Mack Sennett Bathing Beauties for my first talking picture," said DeMille. "One of the girls was Madalynne Fields, whom I thought had a future in pictures. The other was Jane Peters (sic), whom I discharged for a lack of talent...which sometimes prompts even my best friends to

tell me that I'm not the world's greatest talent scout."
On another occasion he said, "I seem to remember telling a
certain young lady a few years ago that she'd never get
anywhere in pictures.   I believe I said that she didn't
take herself serious enough." DeMille and Lombard eventually laughed about an event that, at the time, hurt her
very badly.

The Racketeer (1930)
Pathe.
Director: Howard Higgins
Associate Producer: Ralph Block
Story, Screenplay: Paul Gangelin
Photography: David Abel
Musical Director: Josiah Zuro

Cast

Mahlon Keane   Robert Armstrong
Rhoda   Carol Lombard
Tony   Roland Drew
Millie   Jeanette Loff
Jack   John Loder
Mehaffey   Paul Hurst
Mr. Simpson   Winter Hall
Mrs. Lee   Hedda Hopper

Summary: Lombard's character is diverted from her true
love by the slimy attentions of the title character,
played by Armstrong.   Horribly dated now and a study in
bad acting, direction, and photography. It should by all
rights have killed Carole's career in its tracks.
Somehow, both it and she survived.

The Arizona Kid (1930)
Fox.
Director: Alfred Santell
Screenplay: Ralph Block, Joseph Wright
Story: Ralph Block
Photography: Glen MacWilliams
Film Editor: Paul Weatherwax
Sound Recorder: George Leverett
Running time: 83 minutes

Cast

The Arizona Kid   Warner Baxter
Lorita   Mona Maris
Virginia Hoyt   Carol Lombard
Pulga   Mrs. Soledad Jiminez
Nick Hoyt   Theodore von Eltz
Snakebite Pete   Arthur Stone
Sheriff Andrews   Walter P. Lewis

Summary: Carol as villainess! Such a turnabout raised the
eyebrows of reviewers when they analyzed this popular
western about the title character's adventures, and his
dalliance with the scheming Lombard character, who proves
to be part of a husband-wife confidence team.   The New
York *Times* said, "Carol Lombard is a beautiful girl, but
it is doubtful whether she is suited to the role of
Virginia."

Safety in Numbers (1930)
Paramount.

Director:	Victor Schertzinger
Screenplay:	Marion Dix
Story:	George Marion, Jr.,
	Percy Heath
Photography:	Henry Gerrard
Songs, lyrics:	Marion and Richard Whiting
Dances:	David Bennett
Film Editor:	Robert Bassler
Running time:	78 minutes

Cast

William Butler Reynolds	Charles "Buddy" Rogers
Jacqueline	Kathryn Crawford
Maxine	Joseph Dunn
Pauline	Carol Lombard
Cleo Careine	Geneva Mitchell
Bertram Shipiro	Roscoe Karns
Phil Kempton	Francis McDonald
Alma McGregor	Virginia Bruce
Messaline	Louise Beavers

Summary: Lombard portrays one of three party girls who
squire the naive hero, Rogers, around town. Based on her
work here, Paramount offered her a seven year contract.

Fast and Loose (1930)
Paramount.

Director:	Fred Newmeyer
Screenplay:	Doris Anderson
Dialogue:	Preston Sturges
Play:	David Gray
Photography:	William Steiner
Dialogue Director:	Bertram Harrison
Running time:	87 minutes

Cast

Marion Lenox	Miriam Hopkins
Alice O'Neil	Carole Lombard
Bronson Lenox	Frank Morgan
Henry Morgan	Charles Starrett

Bertie Lenox   Henry Wadsworth
Carrie Lenox   Winifred Harris
George Grafton   Herbert Yost

Summary: Carole is a showgirl who falls in love with a
millionaire's son. Released in November, 1930, its advertising materials spelled *Carol* with an e. This spelling
remained through the rest of her career.

It Pays to Advertise (1931)
Paramount.
Director: Frank Tuttle
Screenplay: Arthur Kober
Play: Roi Cooper Megrue,
                                         Walter Hackett
Photography: Archie J. Stout
Running time: 75 minutes

Cast

Rodney Martin   Norman Foster
Mary Grayson   Carole Lombard
Ambrose Peale   Skeets Gallagher
Cyrus Martin   Eugene Pallette
Adams   Lucien Littlefield
Comtesse de Beaurien   Helen Johnson
Thelma Temple   Louise Brooks
Donald McChesney   Morgan Wallace

Summary: The story, played as comedy, concerns the son of
a soap king who produces an ad campaign for a   nonexistent
product. Lombard portrays the love interest, with popular
silent star Brooks seventh billed in support.

Man of the World (1931)
Paramount.
Director: Richard Wallace
Story, Screenplay: Herman J. Mankiewicz
Photography: Victor Milner
Running time: 71 minutes

Cast

Michael Wagstag   William Powell
Mary Kendall   Carole Lombard
Irene   Wynne Gibson
Harold Taylor   Guy Kibbee
Frank Thompson   Lawrence Gray
Mr. Bradkins   Tom Ricketts

Summary: Powell is a blackmailer, Lombard the girl for
whom he reforms. The script by Mankiewicz provides an
unusual atmosphere and keeps the film moving. This was

the project that brought Lombard and Powell together; they had fallen in love by the end of production.

Ladies' Man (1931)
Paramount.
Director: Lothar Mendes
Screenplay, Dialogue: Herman J. Mankiewicz
Story: Rupert Hughes
Photography: Victor Milner
Running time: 70 minutes

Cast

James Darricott	William Powell
Norma Page	Kay Francis
Rachel Fendley	Carole Lombard
Horace Fendley	Gilbert Emery
Mrs. Fendley	Olive Tell
Anthony Fendley	Martin Burton
Peyton Weldon	John Holland

Summary: Powell is a gigolo-type who specializes in wealthy wives. Lombard is the daughter of one of those wives. Played as comedy throughout, Powell's death at the film's climax ruins the atmosphere created. Carole is overshadowed by leading lady Kay Francis.

Up Pops the Devil (1931)
Paramount.
Director: A. Edward Sutherland
Screenplay: Arthur Kober, Eve Unsell
Play: Albert Hackett,
                                     Francis Goodrich
Photography: Karl Struss
Dialogue: Arthur Kober, Eve Unsell
Running time: 86 minutes

Cast

Biney Hatfield	Skeets Gallagher
Stranger	Stuart Erwin
Anne Merrick	Carole Lombard
Polly Griscom	Lilyan Tashman
Steve Merrick	Norman Foster
George Kent	Edward J. Nugent
Gilbert Morrell	Theodore von Eltz
Luella May Carroll	Joyce Compton

Summary: Now a "lost film" because of legal entanglements, the plot is a Mr. Mom ancestor with Lombard a stage dancer and Foster her novelist husband.

I Take This Woman (1931)
Paramount.

Directors:	Marion Gering,
	Slavko Vorkapich
Screenplay:	Vincent Lawrence
Novel:	Mary Roberts Rinehart
Photography:	Victor Milner
Running time:	73 minutes

Cast

Tom McNair	Gary Cooper
Kay Dowling	Carole Lombard
Aunt Bessie	Helen Ware
Herbert Forrest	Lester Vail
Mr. Dowling	Charles Trowbridge
Sue Barnes	Clara Blandick
Bill Wentworth	Gerald Fielding
Jake Mallory	Albert Hart
Sid	Guy Oliver
Shorty	Syd Taylor
Clara Hammell	Mildred Van Dorn

Summary: Hick cowboy falls for glamous urbanite. Another in Lombard's ongoing string of mediocre productions. She altered her makeup for some scenes, leading *Photoplay* to note, "You'll get a surprise...seeing lovely Carole's beauty sunk as the ranch drudge-of-all-work."

No One Man (1932)
Paramount.

Director:	Lloyd Corrigan
Screenplay:	Sidney Buchman, Percy
	Heath, Agnes Brand Leahy
Story:	Rupert Hughes
Photography:	Charles Lang
Running time:	72 minutes

Cast

Penelope Newbold	Carole Lombard
Bill Hanaway	Ricardo Cortez
Dr. Karl Bemis	Paul Lukas
Sue Folsom	Juliette Compton
Alfred Newbold	George Barbies
Mrs. Newbold	Virginia Hammond
Stanley McIlvaine	Arthur Pierson
Delia	Francis Moffett
License clerk	Irving Bacon

Summary: Carole, as yet another socialite, plays the field before settling on Lukas's character as her mate. Lombard made this film following her Hawaiian honeymoon, at which point she had become ill. Pleurisy followed in mid-pro-

duction; she looks none too healthy as a result.   Her
first starring film, thanks to Myron Selznick's influence,
which is not to say that her road to success was easy from
this point on. *Variety*'s review states: "Miss Lombard, as
the figure around which everything revolves, has a two-way
handicap to overcome for sympathy.   One is the character
she plays and the other is the camera.   The lens has been
none too kind to her here.   Gorgeous in 'stills,' the re-
production on the screen for her is such as to cause audi-
ble unfavorable comments from women in the audience.

Sinners in the Sun (1932)
Paramount.

Director:	Alexander Hall
Screenplay:	Vincent Lawrence, Waldemar Young, Samuel Hoffenstein
Story:	Mildred Crain
Photography:	Ray June
Running time:	71 minutes

Cast

Doris Blake	Carole Lombard
Jimmie Martin	Chester Morris
Claire Kinkaid	Adrienne Ames
Mrs. Blake	Alison Skipworth
Eric Nelson	Walter Byron
Mr. Blake	Reginald Barlow
Mrs. Florence Nelson	Rita LaRoy
Ridgeway	Cary Grant
Grandfather Blake	Luke Cosgrove

Summary: A soap opera that drew moaning responses from
critics, with good reason.   Lombard and Morris play young
lovebirds who argue, break up, and marry other people
only to be reunited by film's end.   During production,
Paramount went bankrupt, heads rolled, and everyone was
miserable.   Cary Grant was just starting his steady climb
to stardom with this film.   He and Carole would soon
become close social friends.

Virtue (1932)
Columbia.

Director:	Edward Buzzell
Screenplay:	Robert Riskin
Story:	Ethel Hill
Photography:	Joseph Walker
Assistant Director:	Sam Nelson
Running time:	87 minutes

Cast

Mae	Carole Lombard

Jimmy	Pat O'Brien
Frank	Ward Bond
MacKenzie	Willard Robertson
Gert	Shirley Grey
Magistrate	Ed LeSaint
Toots/Gunman	Jack LaRue
Girlfriend of Toots	Mayo Methot

Summary: Lombard was loaned to lowly Columbia so that
Paramount could defray the cost of her salary, at least
for a while.   She plays a prostitute reformed by cabby
O'Brien, a role that furthered her career not at all. It
did further her love life, however, as she met and became
infatuated with scriptwriter Riskin during production.

No More Orchids (1932)
Columbia.

Director:	Walter Lang
Screenplay:	Gertrude Purcell
Story:	Grace Perkins
Adaptation:	Keene Thompson
Photography:	Joseph August
Assistant Director:	Sam Nelson
Running time:	72 minutes

Cast

Anne Holt	Carole Lombard
Bill Holt	Walter Connolly
Grandma	Louise Closser Hale
Tony	Lyle Talbot
Dick	Allen Vincent
Rita	Ruthelma Stevens
Cedric	C. Aubrey Smith
Burkhart	William V. Mong
Merriwell	Charles Mailes

Summary: Lombard is a socialite (again) in love with a
pauper (again). The director, Lang, became a close friend
of Carole's and married her best friend, Madalynne Fields.
Meanwhile, the clandestine Lombard-Riskin romance continued off-stage.

No Man of Her Own (1932)
Paramount.

Director:	Wesley Ruggles
Screenplay:	Maurine Watkins,
	Milton Gropper
Story:	Edmund Goulding,
	Benjamin Glazer
Photography:	Leo Tover
Running time:	86 minutes

Cast

Jerry "Babe" Stewart	Clark Gable
Connie Randall	Carole Lombard
Kay Everly	Dorothy Mackaill
Vane	Grant Mitchell
Mr. Randall	George Barbier
Mrs. Randall	Elizabeth Patterson
Dickie Collins	Farrell MacDonald
Willie Randall	Tommy Conlon
Mr. Morton	Walter Walker

Summary: Carole's portrayal of a small town librarian is about as convincing as Gable's representation of a reform-ing swindler. Which is to say, not very. Still, in their only screen teaming, they sizzle together in a sexy film that has Lombard and Dorothy Mackaill parading around in various stages of undress while Gable looks on in appre-ciation.   At this time Clark was thirty-one and Carole twenty-four, and their relationship was still nearly four years away.

From Hell to Heaven (1933)
Paramount.

Director:	Earle C. Kenton
Screenplay:	Percy Heath,
	Sidney Buchman
Story:	Lawrence Hazard
Photography:	Henry Sharp
Running time:	70 minutes

Cast

Colly Tanner	Carole Lombard
Charlie Bayne	Jack Oakie
Joan Burt	Adrienne Ames
Wesley Burt	David Manners
Cuff Billings	Sidney Blackmer
Sonny Lockwood	Verna Hillie
Tommy Tucker	James C. Eagles
Winnie Lloyd	Shirley Grey
Jack Ruby (crook)	Bradley Page
Pop Lockwood (crook)	Walter Walker
Toledo Jones (crook)	Burton Churchill
Steve Wells	Donald Kerr
Sue Wells	Nydia Westman
Mrs. Chadman	Cecil Cunningham

Summary: This easily-recognized and coldly received immi-tation of *Grand Hotel*, with a racetrack setting, has Lombard as the pining girlfriend of Sidney Blackmer.

Supernatural (1933)
Director: Victor Halperin
Screenplay: Harvey Thew, Brian Marlow
Story, adaptation: Garnett Weston
Photography: Arthur Martinelli
Dialogue Director: Sidney Salkow
Running time: 60 minutes

Cast

Roma Courtney	Carole Lombard
Grant Wilson	Randolph Scott
Ruth Rogen	Vivienne Osborne
Paul Bavian	Alan Dinehart
Dr. Houston	H. B. Warner
Madame Gourjan	Beryl Mercer
Robert Hammond	William Farnum
Warden	Willard Robertson
Max	George Burr MacAnnon
John Courtney	Lyman Williams

Summary: Carole's disapproval of *Supernatural* reached volcanic proportions. (See Chapter 4). Its concepts-- ghosts and spirit possession--eluded her, yet today this film stands as an interesting early attempt at now-cliched subjects.   The story involves a fake medium who comes to Lombard claiming to be in contact with her dead twin brother.   From here it moves quickly and darkly, leaving no stone unturned.

The Eagle and the Hawk (1933)
Paramount.
Director: Stuart Walker, Mitchell
                                 Leisen (uncredited)
Screenplay: Bogart Rogers,
                                 Seton I. Miller
Story: John Monk Sanders
Photography: Harry Fishbeck
Running time: 70 minutes

Cast

Jeremiah Young	Fredric March
Henry Crocker	Cary Grant
Mike Richards	Jack Oakie
The Beautiful Lady	Carole Lombard
Major Dunham	Sir Guy Standing
Hogan	Forrester Harvey
John Stevens	Kenneth Howell
Kingsford	Leland Hodgson
Lady Erskine	Virginia Hammond
General	Crawford Kent
Tommy	Douglas Scott
Major Kruppman	Robert Manning

Summary: Set in World War I, this surprisingly adult
anti-war study is a virtual remake of *The Dawn Patrol*
(1930), from its setting at a front line flying station to
its clever irony to its hard-drinking, slowly disinte-
grating main character, played by March.   Lombard, in a
cameo role, appears for eight minutes at the center of a
crisp, involving, masculine morality play that was a step
up from her recent endeavors.

Brief Moment (1933)
Columbia.

Director:	David Burton
Screenplay:	Brian Marlow,
	Edith Fitzgerald
Play:	S. N. Behrman
Photography:	Ted Tetzlaff
Film Editor	Gene Havlick
Assistant Director:	Wilbur McGough
Running time:	72 minutes

Cast

Abby Fane	Carole Lombard
Rodney Deane	Gene Raymond
Harold Sigrift	Monroe Owsley
Franklin Deane	Donald Cook
Steve Walsh	Arthur Hohl
Mr. Deane	Reginald Mason
Count Armand	Jameson Thomas
Mrs. Deane	Theresa Maxwell Conover
Kay Deane	Florence Britton
Joan	Irene Ware
Alfred	Herbert Evans

Summary: Carole is a torch singer and Raymond an aimless
playboy.   Ted Tetzlaff's skillful photography led him to
become Lombard's favorite.   Immediately after the completion of this film, she left Hollywood to divorce William
Powell.

White Woman (1933)
Paramount.

Director:	Stuart Walker
Screenplay:	Samuel Hoffenstein,
	Gladys Lehman
Story:	Norman Reilly Raine,
	Frank Butler
Photography:	Harry Fishbeck
Songs:	Harry Revel, Mack Gordon
Art Directors:	Hans Dreier, Harry Oliver
Running time:	69 minutes

Cast

Horace Prin	Charles Laughton
Judith Denning	Carole Lombard
Ballister	Charles Bickford
David von Eltz	Kent Taylor
Jakey	Percy Kilbride
Fenton	Charles B. Middleton
Hambley	James Bell
Chisholm	Claude King
Mrs. Chisholm	Ethel Griffies
Vaegi	Jimmie Dime
Connors	Marc Lawrence

Summary: Lombard is pulled out of her usual drawing room habitat to play a sexy singer stuck in Malaya with bad guy husband Laughton.   As she had to sing two songs in the film, she brought in heartthrob Russ Columbo, her new love interest, to act as vocal coach.   The chimp utilized here, named Duke, mauled Carole's arm for no apparent reason.

Bolero (1934)
Paramount.

Director:	Wesley Ruggles
Screenplay:	Horace Jackson
Story:	Carey Wilson,
	Kubec Glasmon
Photography:	Leo Tover
Music:	Ralph Rainger
Film Editor:	Hugh Bennett
Running time:	85 minutes

Cast

Raoul De Baere	George Raft
Helen Hathaway	Carole Lombard
Michael De Baere	William Frawley
Leona	Frances Drake
Annette	Sally Rand
Lord Coray	Ray Milland
Lucy	Gloria Shea
Lady D'Argon	Gertrude Michael
Theatre manager	Del Henderson
Hotel manager	Frank G. Dunn
Belgian landlady	Martha Baumattie

Summary: Raft portrays a dancer who, with Lombard, rises to the top of the heap only to crash back to earth. Lombard's role is standard, although in one scene she strips down to a chemise and stockings for a provocative dance number.   Raft and William Frawley, two no-nonsense, tough talking New Yorkers, make for the most incongruous pair of "Belgians" in screen history.

We're Not Dressing (1934)
Paramount.
Director: Norman Taurog
Screenplay: Horace Jackson, Francis
                                    Martin, George Marion
Story: Benjamin Glazer
Photography: Charles Lang
Music, lyrics: Harry Revel, Mack Gordon
Film Editor: Stuart Heisler
Art Directors: Hans Dreier, Ernst Fegte
Running time: 65 minutes

Cast

Stephen Jones   Bing Crosby
Doris Worthington   Carole Lombard
George   George Burns
Gracie   Gracie Allen
Edith   Ethel Merman
Hubert   Leon Errol
Prince Alexander Stofani   Jay Henry
Prince Michael Stofani   Ray Milland
Old Sailor   John Irwin
Captain   Charles Morris

Summary: Based on the novel *The Admirable Crichton* by
James M. Barrie, this musical comedy resembles an excur-
sion into the pros and cons of Vaudeville. With the above
cast all fighting for screen time, shtick oozes everywhere
until Crosby starts singing, at which point the proceedings grind to a halt.   Lombard, not yet a genuine screwball, gets lost in the shuffle.

Twentieth Century (1934)
Columbia.
Director: Howard Hawks
Story, Screenplay: Ben Hecht,
                                    Charles MacArthur
Photography: Joseph August
Film Editor   Gene Havlick
Assistant Director: C. C. Coleman
Running time: 91 minutes

Cast

Oscar Jaffe   John Barrymore
Lily Garland   Carole Lombard
Oliver Webb   Walter Connolly
Owen O'Malley   Roscoe Karns
Max Jacobs   Charles Levison
Clark   Etienne Girardot
Sadie   Dale Fuller
George Smith   Ralph Forbes
Anita   Billie Seward

Lockwood	Clifford Thompson
Conductor	James P. Burtis
Myrtle Schultz	Gigi Parrish
Mr. McGonigle	Edgar Kennedy

Summary: Carole's breakthrough film is the brilliant, lightning-witted story of eccentric Broadway producer Barrymore, who takes shopgirl Lombard and makes her both star and mistress, driving her slightly mad in the process. Filmed in all of five weeks, it marked Lombard's emergence as star and screen personality.

Now and Forever (1934)
Paramount.

Director:	Henry Hathaway
Producer:	Louis D. Lighton
Screenplay:	Vincent Lawrence, Sylvia Thalliery
Story:	Jack Kirkland, Melville Baker
Photography:	Harry Fishbeck
Music, lyrics:	Harry Revel, Mack Gordon
Art Directors:	Hans Dreier, Robert Usher
Running time:	80 minutes

Cast

Jerry Day	Gary Cooper
Toni Carstairs	Carole Lombard
Penelope Day	Shirley Temple
Felix Evans	Sir Guy Standing
Mrs. J. H. P. Crane	Charlotte Granville
James Higginson	Gilbert Emery
Mr. Clark	Henry Kilker
Mr. Ling	Tetsu Komal
Chris Carstairs	Jameson Thomas
Mr. O'Neill	Harry Stubbe
Doctor	Egon Brecker

Summary: The charisma of the three stars carries the day in a vehicle tailor-made for Temple. All interact well, with both Lombard's and Cooper's performances strong. The story concerns the reformation of con man Coop through his ingenuous daughter Shirley, with Lombard the woman who loves them both.

Lady By Choice (1934)
Columbia; a Robert North Production.

Director:	David Burton
Screenplay:	Jo Swerling
Story:	Dwight Taylor
Photography:	Ted Tetzlaff
Film Editor:	Viola Lawrence

Assistant Director: Arthur Black
Running time: 78 minutes

Cast

Alabam' Lee	Carole Lombard
Patricia Patterson (Patsy)	May Robson
Johnny Mills	Roger Pryor
Judge Daly	Walter Connolly
Kendall	Arthur Hohl
Front O'Malley	Raymond Walburn
Brannigan	James Burke
Lucretia	Mariska Aldrich

Summary: Lombard is a fan dancer playing straight woman
to eccentric old May Robson.   Thanks to Carole's increas-
ing popularity,   this film received more recognition than
her earlier work at Paramount. Her love interest is Roger
Pryor, one of Russ Columbo's best friends.   Columbo died
soon after the completion of filming.

The Gay Bride (1934)
MGM.
Director: Jack Conway
Producer: John W. Considine, Jr.
Screenplay: Bella and Samuel Spewack
Story: Charles Francis Coe
Photography: Ray June
Music: Jack Virgil
Film Editor: Frank Sullivan
Art Director: Cedric Gibbons
Running time: 80 minutes

Cast

Mary	Carole Lombard
Office boy	Chester Morris
Mirabelle	ZaSu Pitts
Mickey	Leo Carrillo
Shoots Magiz	Nat Pendleton
Dingle	Sam Hardy
MacPherson	Walter Walker

Summary: Already reeling from Russ Columbo's death,
Lombard went to work at MGM for the only time in her
career.   The resulting film, made by top MGM director
Conway, proved that the gangster cycle had run its course,
only to be revived a few years later by Warner Brothers.

Rumba (1935)
Paramount.
Director: Marion Gering
Screenplay: Howard J. Green

Additional dialogue:	Harry Ruskin, Frank Partas
Story:	Guy Endore, Seena Owen
Photography:	Ted Tetzlaff
Music, lyrics:	Ralph Rainger
Dances:	Veloz and Yolanda
Film Editor:	Hugh Bennett
Art Directors:	Hans Dreier, Robert Usher
Costumes:	Travis Banton
Running time:	77 minutes

Cast

Joe Martin	George Raft
Diana Harrison	Carole Lombard
Flash	Lynne Overman
Carmelita	Margo
Hobart Fletcher	Monroe Owsley
Goldie Allen	Iris Adrian
Henry B. Harrison	Samuel S. Hinds
Mrs. Harrison	Virginia Hammond
Patsy	Gail Patrick
Tony	Akim Tamiroff

Summary: A *Bolero* clone that fooled nobody and in fact drew cries of "foul" from reviewers. Carole plays a socialite who gets mixed up with Raft, a dancer, and is predictably forced to replace his partner for the climactic dance.

Hands Across the Table (1935)
Paramount.

Director:	Mitchell Leisen
Producer:	E. Lloyd Sheldon
Supervision:	Ernst Lubitsch
Screenplay:	Norman Krasna, Vincent Laurence, Herbert Fields
Story:	Vina Delmar
Photography:	Ted Tetzlaff
Music, lyrics:	Sam Caslow, Frederick Hollander
Running time:	81 minutes

Cast

Regi Allen	Carole Lombard
Theodore Drew III	Fred MacMurray
Allen Macklyn	Ralph Bellamy
Vivian Snowden	Astrid Allwyn
Laura	Ruth Donnelly
Nona	Marie Prevost
Peter	Joseph Tozer
Natty	William Demarest
Pinky Kelly	Edward Gargan
Miles	Ferdinand Munier

Valentine   Harold Minjir
French maid   Marcelle Corday

Summary: Lombard, as a manicurist, is trying to golddig
her way to happiness.   MacMurray is a naive and penniless
playboy with the same idea, although he strikes a wealthy
pose and Lombard falls for him.   One of her best, most enduring comedies, it features appealing characters and surprising raciness (single man staying in single woman's
apartment, with tarty humor thrown in).   This was her
first tailored Paramount comedy, her first film with
Leisen as sole director, and her first teaming with Fred
MacMurray.

Love Before Breakfast (1936)
Universal.
Director: Walter Lang
Producer: Edmund Grainger
Screenplay: Herbert Fields
Story: Faith Baldwin
Additional dialogue: Gertrude Princell
Photography: Ted Tetzlaff
Musical Director: Franz Waxman
Film Editor   Maurice Wright
Assistant Director: Phil Karlstein
Art Director: Albert D'Agostino
Gowns: Travis Banton
Running time: 70 minutes

                    Cast

Kay Colby   Carole Lombard
Scott Miller   Preston Foster
Mrs. Colby   Janet Beecher
Bill Wadsworth   Cesar Romero
Contessa Campanella   Betty Lawford
College boy   Douglas Blackley
Stuart Farnum   Don Briggs
Fat Man   Bert Roach
Charles   Andre Beranger
Brinkerhoff   Richard Carle
Captain   E. E. Clive
Junior   Pushface

Summary: It is unclear why Universal would want Lombard
for this thinly plotted comedy concoction about a love
triangle.   She makes it interesting, however, by athleti-
cally riding both a horse and the handlebars of a bicycle,
and by allowing herself to be drenched during several
scenes that comprise the film's climax.   Lombard's cherished, wheezy old pet Pekingese, Pushface, appears as
"Junior."   Their mutual affection is plainly evident.

The Princess Comes Across (1936)
Paramount.

Director:	William K. Howard
Producer:	Arthur Hornblow, Jr.
Screenplay:	Walter De Leon, Francis Martin, Frank Butler, Don Hartman
Story:	Philip MacDonald
Novel:	Louis Lucien Rogers
Photography:	Ted Tetzlaff
Photographic Effects:	Farciot Edouart, Dewey Wrigley
Music, lyrics:	Phil Boutelje, Jack Scholl
Film Editor:	Paul Weatherwax
Assistant Director:	Harry Scott
Running time:	77 minutes

Cast

Princess Olga	Carole Lombard
King Mantell	Fred MacMurray
Lorel	Douglas Dumbrille
Lady Gertrude Allwyn	Alison Skipworth
Benton	William Frawley
Darcy	Porter Hall
Captain Nicholls	George Barbier
Cragg	Lumsden Hare
Steindorf	Sig Ruman
Morevitch	Mischa Auer
Kawati	Tetsu Komai
The Stranger	Bradley Page

Summary: A truly offbeat mixture of comedy and mystery
that manages to sustain itself until the final credits,
the story is set on a luxury liner, with Lombard disguised
as a princess, and MacMurray the bandleader who helps her
out of a murder rap.   Lombard is shown to brilliant advantage when, full of vulnerability, she stumbles upon a body
in her stateroom.   MacMurray and Frawley appear together
some twenty-three years before *My Three Sons*.

My Man Godfrey (1936)
Universal.

Director:	Gregory LaCava
Screenplay:	Morrie Ryskind, Eric Hatch
Novel:	Eric Hatch
Photography:	Ted Tetzlaff
Music:	Charles Previn
Film Editor:	Ted Kent
Film Supervisor:	Maurice Pivar
Assistant Director:	Scott R. Beal
Art Director:	Charles D. Hall

Cast

Godfrey Parke	William Powell

Irene Bullock	Carole Lombard
Angelica Bullock	Alice Brady
Cornelia Bullock	Gail Patrick
Molly	Jean Dixon
Alexander Bullock	Eugene Pallette
Tommy Gray	Alan Mowbray
Carlo	Mischa Auer
Faithful George	Robert Light
Mike	Pat Flaherty
Master of Ceremonies	Franklin Pagborn
Van Rumple	Grady Sutton
Detective	Ed Gargan
Second Detective	James Flavin
Doorman	Robert Perry

Summary: The definitive screwball comedy, of a sane butler in a houseful of zanies, received Academy Award nomi-
nations for actor and actress (Powell and Lombard),   sup-
porting actor and actress (Auer and Brady), and director
(LaCava).   It remains today as fresh and timeless as the
day it was made, and offers Lombard's finest comedic performance. For the last time in her career she surrendered
top billing in order to play a part, and she considered
this role her most difficult.   A then-novel concept was
utilized for this film as it was shot "off the cuff,"
with dialogue made up on the set as the action progressed.

Swing High, Swing Low (1937)
Paramount.

Director:	Mitchell Leisen
Screenplay:	Virginia Van Upp, Oscar Hammerstein II
Play:	George Manker Watters, Arthur Hopkins
Photography:	Ted Tetzlaff
Photographic Effects:	Farciot Edouart
Musical Director:	Boris Morros
Film Editor:	Edna Warren
Assistant Director:	Edgar Anderson
Art Directors:	Hans Dreier, Ernst Fegte
Costumes:	Travis Banton

Cast

Maggie King	Carole Lombard
Skid Johnson	Fred MacMurray
Harry	Charles Butterworth
Ella	Jean Dixon
Anita Alvarez	Dorothy Lamour
Harvey Dexter	Harvey Stephens
Murphy	Cecil Cunningham
Georgie	Charlie Arnt
Henri	Franklin Pangborn
The Don	Anthony Quinn

Lombard and Powell in **My Man Godfrey**, 1936. (Photo courtesy of John McElwee.)

The Purser   Bug Flanagan
Tony   Charles Judels

Summary: A mean-spirited, weakly scripted comedy drama
set down Panama-way, with MacMurray a no-good trumpet
player and Lombard an unworthy entertainer.   Contrivance
follows contrivance in a film that seems far longer than
its running time, yet it somehow became a top-grossing
hit.   Two Lombard highlights: she adequately sings two
songs, and she continued to defy the Production Code by
going braless.

Nothing Sacred (1937)
Selznick-International; released through United Artists.
Director: William Wellman
Producer: David O. Selznick
Screenplay: Ben Hecht
Story: William Street
Photography: W. Howard Greene
Photographic Effects: Jack Cosgrove
Musical Score: Oscar Levant
Film Editor: James E. Newcom
Assistant Director: Frederick A. Spencer
Art Director: Lyle Wheeler
Costumes: Travis Banton,
                                     Walter Plunkett
Color: Technicolor
Running time: 77 minutes

                        Cast

Hazel Flagg   Carole Lombard
Wally Cook   Fredric March
Dr. Downer   Charles Winninger
Stone   Walter Connolly
Dr. Eggelhoffer   Sig Ruman
Master of Ceremonies   Frank Fay
Max   Maxie Rosenbloom
Dr. Kerchinwisser   Alex Schoenberg
Dr. Vunch   Monte Woolley
Dr. Marachuffsky   Alex Novinsky
Drug Store Lady   Margaret Hamilton
Ernest Walker   Troy Brown
Mrs. Walker   Hattie McDaniel
Dr. Donner's Nurse   Katherine Shelton
Baggage Man   Olin Howland
Wrestler   Ben Morgan
Wrestler   Hans Steinke

Summary: Selznick's character assassination of New York
City and the newspaper world is relentlessly clever but
rarely hilarious.   Lombard's performance is effectively
restrained, and her chemistry with the affable March
proved quite correct.   Best scenes: March knocking out

Lombard with a punch to the jaw, and then Lombard return-
ing the favor. This was Carole's only feature-length
Technicolor appearance, and remains one of her most popular films.

True Confession (1937)
Paramount.

Director:	Wesley Ruggles
Producer:	Albert Lewin
Screenplay:	Claude Binyon
Play:	Louis Verneuil, Georges Berr
Photography:	Ted Tetzlaff
Musical Director:	Boris Morros
Musical Score:	Frederick Hollander
Film Editor:	Paul Weatherwax
Art Director:	Hans Dreier, Robert Usher
Costumes:	Travis Banton

Cast

Helen Bartlett	Carole Lombard
Kenneth Bartlett	Fred MacMurray
Charley	John Barrymore
Daisy McClure	Una Merkel
Prosecutor	Porter Hall
Darsey	Edgar Kennedy
Bartender	Lynne Overman
Krayler's Butler	Fritz Field
Judge	Richard Carle
Otto Krayler	John T. Murray
Typewriter Man	Tommy Dugan
Tony Krauch	Garry Owen
Suzanne Baggart	Toby Wing
Ella	Hattie McDaniel
Pedestrian	Bernard Suss

Summary: Lombard's last Paramount film reflected her entire career there: unsatisfying. It contains unappealing
characters, disrupted pacing thanks to the insertion of a
repugnant John Barrymore character, and generally proved
that Lombard's talent had its limits; she virtually produced the film and made all the wrong decisions herself.

Fools for Scandal (1938)
Warner Brothers.

Director, Producer:	Mervyn Le Roy
Screenplay:	Herbert and Joseph Fields
Additional Dialogue:	Irving Beecher
Play:	Nancy Hamilton, James Shute, Rosemary Casey
Photography:	Ted Tetzlaff
Musical Director:	Leo F. Forbstein

Music, lyrics: Richard Rogers,
                                       Lorens Hart
Film Editor: William Holmes
Art Director: Anton Grot
Miss Lombard's Gowns: Travis Banton
Running time: 82 minutes

Cast

Kay Winters   Carole Lombard
Rene   Fernand Gravet
Phillip Chester   Ralph Bellamy
Dewey Gibson   Allen Jenkins
Lady Paula Malveston   Isabel Jeans
Myrtle   Marie Wilson
Jill   Marcia Ralston
Agnes   Tola Nesmith
Lady Potter-Porter   Heather Thatcher
Papa   Jacques Lory

Summary: Lombard's Waterloo of comedy. This film about
the romance between a Frenchman and American film star was
a critical and commercial disaster for several excellent
reasons. It had all-star people at the skill positions
yet emerged boring and unfunny, with no character development and clumsy, amateurish direction. In mid-movie,
Lombard and Gravet embarrassingly break into song; the
Photoplay reviewer couldn't decide whether to call it
"inane" or "pointless," so he used both.

Made for Each Other (1939)
Selznick-Internationa;; released through United Artists.
Director: John Cromwell
Producer: David O. Selznick
Production Designer: William Cameron Menzies
Photography: Leon Shamroy
Photographic Effects: Jack Cosgrove
Musical Score: Lou Forbes
Film Editor: James E. Newcom
Assistant Director: Eric Stacey
Art Director: Lyle Wheeler
Costumes: Travis Banton

Cast

Jane Mason   Carole Lombard
John Mason   James Stewart
Judge Doolittle   Charles Coburn
Mrs. Mason   Lucile Watson
Conway   Eddie Quillan
Sister Madeline   Alma Kruger
Eunice Doolittle   Ruth Weston
Carter   Donald Briggs
Dr. Healy   Harry Davenport

*Lombard and Fredric March in **Nothing Sacred**, 1937.*

Lilly	Louise Beavers
First Cook	Esther Dale
Second Cook	Renee Orsell
Hatton	Ward Bond
Farmer	Olin Howland
Farmer's Wife	Ferm Emmett
John Mason, Jr. (newly born)	Bonnie Belle Barber
John Mason, Jr. (one year old)	Jackie Taylor

Summary: The ads read, "Carole cries!" and this indeed indicates the career alterations she made in the wake of recent setbacks.   Selznick was at this time involved with *Gone With the Wind* pre-production and   therefore   stripped the Lombard-Stewart film down to an economical modern set-ting.   The story concerns the struggles of a young pair of newlyweds   and is highly competent,   if not highly   enter-taining.

In Name Only (1939)
RKO Radio.

Director:	John Cromwell
Producer:	George Haight
Screenplay:	Richard Sherman
Novel:	Bessie Brewer
Photography:	J. Roy Hunt
Musical Score:	Roy Webb
Film Editor:	William Hamilton
Assistant Director:	Dewey Starkey
Art Director:	Van Nest Polglase
Miss Lombard's Gowns:	Irene
Running time:	102 minutes

Cast

Julie Eden	Carole Lombard
Alec Walker	Cary Grant
Maida Walker	Kay Francis
Mr. Walker	Charles Coburn
Suzanne	Helen Vinson
Laura	Katharine Alexander
Dr. Gateson	Jonathon Hale
Dr. Muller	Maurice Moscovitch
Mrs. Walker	Nella Walker
Ellen	Peggy Ann Garner
Gardner	Spencer Charters

Summary: Originally entitled *Memory of Love,* this somber soap opera concerns the loveless marriage of Grant and Francis, with Lombard tossed in as the "other woman."   She had played this role in real life with Clark and Ria Gable and knew it well.   As for the casting of Francis, this was Lombard's attempt to salvage her friend's sunken career and self-respect.   It worked only temporarily.

Vigil in the Night (1940)
RKO Radio.

Director, Producer:	George Stevens
Screenplay:	Fred Guidl, P. J. Wolfson, Rowland Leigh
Novel:	A. J. Cronin
Photography:	Robert de Grasse
Musical Score:	Alfred Newman
Film Editor:	Henry Berman
Assistant Director:	Syd Fogel
Art Director:	Van Nest Polglase
Associate Art Director:	L. P. Williams
Costumes:	Walter Plunkett
Running time:	96 minutes

Cast

Anne Lee	Carole Lombard
Dr. Prescott	Brian Aherne
Lucy Lee	Anne Shirley
Matthew Bowley	Julien Mitchell
Dr. Caley	Robert Coote
Nora	Brenda Forbes
Glennie	Rita Page
Joe Shand	Peter Cushing
Matron East	Ethel Griffies
Mrs. Bowley	Doris Lloyd
Sister Gilson	Emily Fitzroy

Summary: Lombard's third straight dramatic effort was
calculated to be a career acting achievement, not a big
money-maker.   It failed on both counts thanks to a script
that offered unrelenting gloom but no real insight into
Lombard's character of a noble nurse.   Coming off her ap-
pendectomy--or miscarriage--her performance is indeed a
quiet one.   Audiences weren't interested in an hour and a
half of suffering, and the film lost nearly $300,000.

They Knew What They Wanted (1940)
RKO Radio.

Director:	Garson Kanin
Producer:	Erich Pommer
Executive Producer:	Harry E. Edington
Screenplay:	Robert Ardrey
Play:	Sidney Howard
Photography:	Harry Stradling
Special Effects:	Vernon L. Walker
Musical Score:	Alfred Newman
Film Editor:	John Sturges
Assistant Director:	Ruby Rosenberg
Art Director:	Van Nest Polglase
Costumes:	Edward Stevenson
Running time:	96 minutes

Cast

Amy Peters	Carole Lombard
Tony Patucci	Charles Laughton
Joe	William Gargan
The Doctor	Harry Carey
Father McKee	Frank Fay
The R. F. D.	Joe Bernard
Mildred	Janet Fox
Ah Gee	Lee Tung-Foo
Red	Karl Malden
The Photographer	Victor Kilian
Hired Hand	Paul Lepers

Summary: Arguably Lombard's finest dramatic achievement, a performance of subtlety and great depth that deserved better surroundings.   She portrays a waitress who virtually becomes a mail-order bride for a backward Italian farmer played by Laughton.   Laughton detested Lombard and the production of this film was an intensely unhappy one. The result is a broad, stereotyped Charles Laughton performance that may well have escalated Italian-American hostilities prior to World War II.

Mr. and Mrs. Smith (1941)
RKO Radio.

Director:	Alfred Hitchcock
Executive Producer:	Harry E. Edington
Story, Screenplay:	Norman Krasna
Photography:	Harry Stradling
Photographic Effects:	Vernon L. Walker
Musical Score:	Edward Ward
Film Editor:	William Hamilton
Art Director:	Van Nest Polglase
Running Time:	95 minutes

Cast

Ann Smith	Carole Lombard
David Smith	Robert Montgomery
Jeff Custer	Gene Raymond
Chuck Benson	Jack Carson
Mr. Custer	Philip Merivale
Mrs. Custer	Lucile Watson
Sammy	William Tracy
Mr. Deever	Charles Halton
Mrs. Krausheimer	Esther Dale
Martha	Emma Dunn
Proprietor of Lucy's	William Edmunds
Gertie	Betty Compson
Gloria	Patricia Farr
Lily	Adele Pearce

Summary: Carole's   first comedy in three years   involved

the complications of a young married couple who find out
that technically, they aren't married at all. Originally,
Cary Grant was supposed to play the Montgomery role, and
this unfortunate change away from Grant rendered the film
more impotent than it should have been. Hitchcock would
claim that he merely followed the screenplay as described,
yet he did leave his mark on the film. In a shot under the
breakfast table, showing Lombard playing footsy with Montgomery, Carole registers disappointment by letting her
feet sag to the floor. Another scene shows Montgomery
exiting and closing a sliding door, with the camera remaining fixed on that door as we hear the sharp sound of
breaking glass, signifying that Lombard has just thrown a
vase at him. Then there is the scene at the World's Fair
containing a shot of the crowd *far* down below, taken from
an amusement ride and meant to stir up a little virtigo in
the audience, what with the camera shaking so there can be
no sense os equilibrium. It is quite a watchable film,
and the Lombard-Gene Raymond scenes stand out.

To Be or Not to Be (1942)
United Artists.

Director, Producer:	Ernst Lubitsch
Screenplay:	Edwin Justus Mayer
Story:	Ernst Lubitsch,
	Melchior Lengyel
Photography:	Rudolph Mate
Photographic Effects:	Lawrence Butler
Musical Score:	Werner Heyman
Film Editor:	Dorothy Spencer
Art Director:	Vincent Korda
Running time:	100 minutes

Cast

Maria Tura	Carole Lombard
Joseph Tura	Jack Benny
Lieutenant Stanislav Sobinski	Robert Stack
Greenberg	Felix Bressart
Rawitch	Lionel Atwill
Professor Siletsky	Stanley Ridges
Colonel Ehrhardt	Sig Ruman
Bronski	Tom Dugan
Dobosh	Charles Halton
Captain Schulz	Henry Victor
Anna	Maude Eburne

Summary: Carole's last film may also be her best, an uneasy blend of comedy and tense drama that works on all
cylinders. The story concerns a Polish acting company in
Nazi-occupied Warsaw. This was her happiest acting experience in years, until the bombing of Pearl Harbor, which
occurred near the end of production. Anti-Nazi films were
considered quite daring at this time, and the edginess of

the performances reflect this fact.   When released, the film failed to capture public interest, partly because of the subject matter, and partly because the nation could find little pleasure in the posthumous performance of such a tragic figure.   The critical response has, however, re-mained amazingly consistent through the years. *Time* com-mended it for "deftly ridiculing Hitler and the Nazis." *Photoplay* said, "The last picture made by Carole Lombard remains a fitting tribute to the vital, arresting beauty and personality of the star."   Thirty years later, film historian Leonard Maltin would be moved to write, "The finished film is...a brilliant topical comedy whose wisdom and humor transcend the passage of years to make it as effective in the seventies as it was in 1942."

RADIO APPEARANCES

My Man Godfrey
CBS; Lux Radio Theatre, 9 May 1938

Cast

Godfrey Parke	William Powell
Irene Bullock	Carole Lombard
Cornelia Bullock	Gail Patrick
Carlo	Mischa Auer
Tommy Gray	David Niven
Alexander Bullock	Wallace Clark

Summary: A year after Lombard and Powell filmed *My Man Godfrey,* the death of Jean Harlow threw Powell into a bout of extreme depression and soon, he was diagnosed as suf-fering from rectal cancer. The resulting surgery laid him low for nearly another year, and he was just making his comeback at the time of this radio broadcast. Lombard had helped see him through these emotional crises, and as with all of her appearances at the CBS Playhouse Theatre, she made the evening an event.   After the radio play had been broadcast, she led everyone across Vine Street to the Brown Derby, her favorite restaurant.   This particular broadcast featured an admission from host Cecil B. DeMille that he had made a mistake in "discharging" Lombard from the film *Dynamite.*   In addition, he interviewed Madalynne Fields about the off-screen Lombard.

The Circle
NBC, 15 January-5 February 1939

Cast: Ronald Colman, Carole Lombard, Cary Grant, Groucho Marx, Chico Marx.

Summary: The sponsor of this unorthodox venture, Kel-logg's Corn Flakes, took a $2 million dollar bath on six

months' worth of weekly Sunday night shows. Carole
stuck around for exactly four weeks, earning $5,000 per
week in a series that featured scripted discussions about
all aspects of life and the arts, as well as bouts of
musical entertainment. Ranging from interesting to embar-
rassing in turn, it would have fared much better without
the scripts, with the stars "winging it."

Tailored by Toni
Gulf Screen Guild Show, 12 March 1939

Cast

Toni Warren	Carole Lombard
Peter Graham	James Stewart
Mrs. Warren	Spring Byington
Kenneth Pickles	Edward Everett Horton

Summary: Toni Warren, New York's foremost designer of
men's clothes, visits Greenwich Village to find a shabbily
dressed artist she can make over and present as a Toni
Warren creation. She stumbles on struggling playwright
Peter Graham and after a few hours together, he proposes
to her. He soon becomes successful and falls for the star
of his play, causing Toni to seek a Reno divorce. Before
this can happen, however, Toni and Peter are reunited.
She decides to give up her career so they can move to Ver-
mont and live happily ever after.

In Name Only
CBS; Lux Radio Theatre, 11 December 1939

Cast

Julie Eden	Carole Lombard
Alec Walker	Cary Grant
Maida Walker	Kay Francis

Summary: A lackluster radio version of a lackluster film.

Made for Each Other
CBS; Lux Radio Theatre, 19 February 1940

Cast

Jane Mason	Carole Lombard
John Mason	Fred MacMurray

Summary: Three years after their last joint project,
Lombard and MacMurray teamed up one last time for this re-
creation of the 1939 Lombard-Stewart film.

The Awful Truth
The Gulf Screen Guild Theatre, 17 May 1940

Cast

Lucy Warriner	Carole Lombard
Jerry Warriner	Robert Young
Dan Leeson	Ralph Bellamy

Summary: Only Ralph Bellamy repeats his role from the popular 1937 film version, with Carole taking over for Irene Dunne, and Robert Young assuming the Cary Grant role.   The Gulf Screen Guild host, Roger Pryor, had co-starred with Lombard in the 1934 film *Lady By Choice*, and had been one of Russ Columbo's close friends.

The Moon's Our Home
CBS;Lux Radio Theatre, 10 February 1941

Cast

Cherry Chester	Carole Lombard
Anthony Amberton	James Stewart

Summary: A full five years elapsed between the film and radio versions of this contrived story centering around the relationship of movie actress Chester and author Amberton.   Margaret Sullivan and Henry Fonda had starred on-screen.

Mr. and Mrs. Smith
CBS;Lux Radio Theatre, 9 June 1941

Cast

Ann Smith	Carole Lombard
David Smith	Bob Hope
Chuck Benson	Bill Goodwin
Jeff Custer	Jack Arnold

Summary: After listening to Hope--Mr. Comic Timing--as David Smith, one can only wonder at the possibilities, had he been cast in the film version.   For that matter, any Lombard-Hope teaming might have been gold, as they clearly shared the right chemistry.   Hope's banter after the end of the play is hilarious; better than the play itself.

4. The Complete Lombard

Included in this chapter are several items intended to help round out the character of Carole Lombard as regards her life and times, her sense of humor, her writing style, and the personality that emerged through interviews.

Of particular interest are the four reprinted items. The 1938 *Hollywood Reporter* article is a rare example of the Lombard writing style, and shows the workings of a clear, sharp mind that may one day have risen to studio presidency, except for a certain plane ride taken on a certain January day.

Two reprints are fan magazine articles which, taken together, give a well-rounded look at the essense of Carole Lombard, her philosophies, and her sense of good will. She was known as the most generous woman in Hollywood, thanks to the 1925 automobile accident that left her extremely empathic with anyone given a bad break. The article entitled "Why Is Carole Lombard Hiding Out from Hollywood?" may sound like pablum at first blush, owing to the writer's style, but the substance of the piece is solid, as is the research. Take the case of one-legged Pat Drew, or stand-in Betty Hall. Or Alice Marble. Or Margaret Tallichet. All true, all easily verified.

As for "Lombard--As She Sees Herself," no finer interview was ever conducted with a 1930s star. Soon after Carole sat down with writer Gladys Hall, something clicked and the session became magic. Her language was heavily censored, but her enthusiasm for life, and her ambitions, come shining through. For example, it is revealed here that she was actively seeking her "dream house" in the San Fernando Valley months before she and Gable had bought Raoul Walsh's ranch. Most moving are her allusions to a fear of heights, and her viewpoint on growing older.

The fourth reprint, the C. A. B. report on the crash of Flight 3, is also extremely rare in that copies of such documents are not maintained by the Air Force or National Transportation Safety Board. This copy was obtained from the National Archives and is one of the last in existence.

The circumstances of the crash are somewhat peculiar;

for example, the pilot was cleared to fly *contact*, by sight rather than by instruments, from Las Vegas to Burbank, and that on a clear, starry night he still failed to distinguish the approaching Potosi Mountain, which amounted to the highest peak anywhere along the flight path.

It seems possible although unlikely that the plane may have been sabotaged in some way based on circumstantial evidence: Lombard was set to attend the premiere of *To Be or Not to Be* two days after the plane crash. This film was the last of Hollywood's pre-war attacks on Nazi Germany, and a previous anti-Nazi film, *The Mortal Storm*, had drawn death threats to the cast during production. (See source no. 035). It was six weeks after Pearl Harbor, at a time when German Fifth Column operatives had yet to be ferreted out. In addition, Lombard was on a government mission at the time of the crash, traveling with fifteen Army Ferrying Command pilots. The captain of Flight 3 was a 12,000 hour veteran with solid experience at night flying. And the radio wave signal would have made it impossible to fly off-course, had either pilot been wearing his headset.

Given all these facts, the Civil Aeronautics Board still felt comfortable with its conclusions, and since the time these conclusions were reached, no challenge to their validity has ever been offered. In all likelihood, human error, mixed with a volatile combination of irony and fate, led to utter disaster for TWA Flight 3 and all aboard.

THE STRANGE DEATH OF RUSS COLUMBO

Three profound turning points marked the adult life of Carole Lombard. The first was the automobile accident of 1925; the second the shooting death of fiance Russ Columbo; the third the beginning of her relationship with Clark Gable in 1936. Much has been written about the accident, its affects and aftermath, and a seemingly end-less stream of information surrounds the Lombard-Gable ro-mance. The very strange death of Columbo, however, has not been carefully explored in a generation where the "Singing Romeo" has been all but forgotten.

Lombard biographer Larry Swindell said of Carole Lombard and Russ Columbo: "She called him the great love of her life. Fielding that reference several years later, an interviewer from *Life* said, 'Of course you mean other than Clark Gable, don't you, Miss Lombard?' Carole...said almost grimly, 'Russ Columbo was *the* great love of my life...and that very definitely is off the record.'" (See source no. 036).

So here we have a man of immense importance in the existence of Carole Lombard, a man whose sudden death at age twenty-six shocked her, outraged her, shattered her in its utter pointlessness.

Russ Columbo exuded charisma. Born Ruggiero de Rudolpho Columbo on January 14, 1908, he had been a child prodigy on the violin and showed such promise that he dropped out of high school to pursue his first love. Ironically, despite his virtuosity he would not gain wide fame until he had shoved his violin into the background to become the vocalist for Gus Arnheim's orchestra at the Cocoanut Grove nightclub in Los Angeles, where he crossed paths with Carole Lombard for the first time. He stumbled upon her again a few years later when both were cast in DeMille's *Dynamite*, although Lombard was soon fired from the production.

Columbo went on to appear in three other films and by 1931 he had become, according to the New York *Times*, "the best of the sob ballad singers." Soon he was churning out four hit records a month and raking in thousands, and an ersatz rivalry with Bing Crosby, dubbed "the Battle of the Baritones," was created to fuel Columbo's reputation.

He returned to Los Angeles from New York in 1933 and began singing at the Silver Slipper nightclub, where Lom-bard feasted her eyes on him in September, 1933, and fell in love. Columbo claimed the feeling was mutual, although he had *been around* in his time, possessed a deadly roving eye, and continued to be romantically linked to, among others, Loretta Young, her sister Sally Blane, and recent Miss America Dorothy Dell. Perhaps Carole was a bit naive in allowing the relationship to deepen, but deepen it did until they began speaking seriously of marriage.

"He told me once that his love for me was the most important thing in his life," said Lombard. "I really be-lieve it was paramount in his thoughts; it even dwarfed

Carole Lombard with Russ Columbo, 1934. (Photo from the collection of Susan Marie Rice.)

his desire for fame and recognition." (See source no. 101).

They were together for exactly one year, until the fateful day of Sunday, September 2, 1934. Carole was near collapse after months of constant work and had gone to Big Bear with Fieldsie to collect herself before beginning her next film, *The Gay Bride,* at MGM. Russ was still riding an emotional high after the successful premiere of his first starring film, *Wake Up and Dream,* although the couple had been experiencing vague worries for weeks.

"Russ and I felt something cataclysmic hanging over us," Lombard told reporter Sonia Lee. "We were depressed without knowing why. Russ was afraid that something was going to happen to me. I had been going from one picture to another, and I was frightfully tired."

With Carole out of town, Russ visited his best friend, photographer Lansing Brown, in Brown's small Hollywood bungalow at 584 Lillian Way. Supposedly Columbo wanted Brown's opinion of *Wake Up and Dream*. Carole said that "Russ depended on Lansing's judgement and considered his criticism extremely valuable."

Lansing Brown owned a collection of antique pistols and was fidgeting with one while speaking to Columbo. Suddenly the gun discharged and in the next instant, Russ was near death, shot through the eye. Or so the story went.

Brown's parents were visiting the house at the time of the shooting and came running when they heard the explosion. They called police, who then called the coroner, thinking Columbo already dead. He wasn't. He clung to life by a thread for hours, making brain surgery necessary. After he was pronounced dead on the table, operating surgeon Dr. George W. Patterson told reporters, "X-ray pictures showed that the bullet had entered the orbit of the left eye and pushed through the center of the brain to the back of the skull, causing a fracture."

Patterson had contacted Lombard at Big Bear before surgery began, but told Carole that the situation was hopeless. She and Fieldsie started back for Hollywood and, Carole said, "I knew on the way down the very instant Russ died. My dog, which loved Russ, was sitting in the back of the car. Suddenly he began to whimper. He crawled over to me and put his muzzle against my neck. Later I checked on the time--Russ had died in that very second."

Carole arrived at the hospital in time to see her supposed friend Sally Blane stealing the spotlight tearfully, telling reporters, "I think he was the first boyfriend of a million girls who saw in him an ideal. I used to go to the Grove just to sit and stare at the boy whose soft voice made one dream. And then I met him. That was about six years ago. He was everything that an ideal should be. Our introduction grew into a warm and understanding friendship that I have prized more than any other possession."

Carole withdrew into a shell and refused to talk to reporters.   At the same time, police grilled Lansing Brown, who stuck to the same improbable story.

The New York *Times* quoted him as saying, "During my entire conversation with Russ, I was absent-mindedly fooling with one of the guns.   I was pulling back the trigger and clicking it, time after time.   I had a match in my left hand and when I clicked, evidently the match caught in between the hammer and the firing pin.   There was an explosion. Russ slid to the side of his chair. I thought he was clowning.   It was all mighty fast.   I called my mother and father, who were in another room. Immediately my father called the police.

"I have had this collection of pistols for seven years.   I bought them at an antiques store.   I have always kept them on top of my desk here.   I had never made an examination of the guns to see if they were loaded, because they were so old.   I had no idea at all they were loaded." (The New York *Times*, 4 September 1934).

Brown's story seemed *too* ridiculous--a match and pistol in the same hand?   In different hands, held close together?   The police, however, couldn't come up with anything better.   A servant reported that Brown and Columbo had been arguing, but Brown had no apparent motive for killing Columbo, unless perhaps the men were quarreling over a woman--a definite possibility considering Russ's romantic exploits.   The situation grew somewhat less vague when detectives checking the den found the mark of a ricochet, where the musket ball had bounced before striking Columbo.   Even a trick marksman would have found such a shot impossible.

Lombard had known Lansing Brown for a few years. Brown had often photographed her and had even taken portraits of Bessie Peters.   Carole accepted Lansing's story at face value, no questions asked.

"Russ and Lansing and I had toyed with those two old dueling pistols a hundred times," she said.   "We poked our fingers into the barrels and held them up to our eyes to squint up into them.   Yet nothing had ever happened.   We never dreamed they were loaded." (See source no. 101).

As with all Hollywood mysteries, rumors rapidly spread and fanned themselves.   Most prominent of these was the assertion that Columbo's death was a Mafia execution.   But what about the ricochet mark?   No hypothesis could be formulated that tied in the Mafia, although twenty years later Albert Columbo, Russ's older brother, was murdered in a way that more strongly hinted at Mafia involvement.   Coincidence?   Probably.   Lombard would have said so at any rate; Lombard felt that fate had dealt Russ Columbo a bum hand, and she wasn't afraid to expound on this idea: "The whole tragedy seems to have been a chain of circumstances leading to death...I am certain that no matter what we might have done, Russ would have died that day." (See source no. 101).

She took comfort in the fact that since she was so

certain that "his number was up," at least he had died while he was "in full bloom." This became a theme in her life--it was best to exit while you were on top rather than much later, when fame and beauty had grown elusive. She said of Russ's death, "I am glad that it came when he was so happy--so happy in our love and in his winning of stardom. That knowledge is a consolation."

Despite her enviable rationalizations, she still drew unwanted scrutiny at Russ's funeral. She hated funerals and almost didn't attend. Soon after the service began she broke down; she went right on crying as she left the church flanked by her mother and brother Stuart.

Understanding as she did the similar grief that Lansing Brown must have been experiencing, she sought him out and told him, "I know you loved Russ. I don't blame you. It was an accident. Russ would want us to go on being friendly, and of course we will." (See source no. 024). The police eventually reached the same conclusion: the shooting of Russ Columbo was a bizarre accident. No formal charges were filed against Lansing Brown. Brown, despite his exoneration, became a tragic, brooding Hollywood figure who would never allow himself to forget what had happened at his hand.

A few weeks after the tragedy, Carole said, "I am desperately lonely for Russ. We were so very close--together so constantly. I'm just beginning to feel the loss. I feel as though I were suspended in air, only slowly coming alive." (See source no. 101).

Russ Columbo left a void in the heart of Carole Lombard that would never be filled. She would go through a line of lovers in the coming year--Robert Riskin, George Raft, Cesar Romero--before she found Clark Gable and proceeded to spend a great deal of her time working like hell to make their relationship work. Judging by her comment to the *Life* reporter in 1938, Clark Gable would never take Russ Columbo's place--*off the record*. *On* the record, Carole and Clark were America's perfect couple, and *this* was the image Lombard was determined to foster. And then Lombard died, presumably as she would have wanted to, in full bloom.

Today, in the Sanctuary of Vespers hallway of Forest Lawn's Great Mausoleum, a high wall vault bears a bronze marker that reads, *Russ Columbo 1908-1934*. A simple inscription for a man who died anything but simply. A room away, almost within sight, is another wall vault containing the remains of Carole Lombard. She rests next to Clark Gable, but Columbo is there watching. And still the mystery lingers as it will always linger, and speculation persists as it will always persist, and no one will ever know exactly what was, and what might have been.

THE LOMBARD WIT

The following are examples, year by year, of Lombard's idea of what was funny; this sense of humor, renowned as it was, formed the basis for her enduring legend.

1933

Part of the filming of *From Hell to Heaven,* a horse-racing opus that would soon bomb at the boxoffice, took place at the Santa Anita racetrack, with Lombard sporting summer attire in mid-January. After a couple of hours of shivering, she grew contemptuous of the snugly dressed crew surrounding her, *behind* the cameras.

"All right, you warm, bloody bastard," she yelled suddenly, "what's good for one is good for all! I'm not shooting till I see every one of you down to your jockey shorts." They complied, much to Carole's delight. (See source no. 029).

The film *Supernatural* was created by the Halperin brothers, Victor and Edward, two cases of arrested development who had just made that weird but talked about *White Zombie*. Encouraged, they filled *Supernatural* with ghosts, possessions, stormy nights, corpses, blackmail and double-crosses. Victor Halperin directed the film himself, and in such an inept manner that Lombard began making statements like, "This guy ought to be running a deli," and "Who do you have to screw to get off this picture?"

Sidney Salkow, who would one day direct over fifty motion pictures, worked as a production assistant on the film and offered this account of Lombard's *Supernatural* actions:

> Matters were not helped when Halperin, a sweet mild-mannered gentleman, consistently managed to place Carole on the wrong side of the camera, revealing her scar. Poor Victor, subject to Carole's pithy and never-ending verbal assaults from morn till night, seemingly could no longer tell her right side from her left. Each time he bumbled, Carole would erupt.
>
> Particularly painful to both Victor and Carole were those times when facial transformations had to be filmed. It was a painstaking process that required Carole to remain motionless for what seemed an eternity while the transformation was achieved with makeup and stop-frame photography. For Carole, whose internal combustion machine was never at rest, this was the final indignity. She came down hard on Victor. "God, this bastard's trying to paralyze me. Victor, God'll punish you for

this...," she moaned.

And maybe God was listening. At 5:10 P.M., March 10, 1933, the set suddenly started to rumble; a deep roar drowned out the clatter of lights, props, furniture, and sets rattling and crashing while the ground swayed and the earth buckled and writhed. In panic everyone ran shrieking from the set in wild flight.

To all of us it was the Long Beach earthquake (it took fifty-two lives). To Carole it was "Lombard's Revenge." I watched her, mindless of everyone's preoccupation with the moment, stride to Victor Halperin huddled outside the still-swaying stage and point a finger at him. "Victor--*that* was only a warning!" (See source no. 029).

1934

The story of *We're Not Dressing* concerned a wacky group of shipwrecked people and called for location shooting at Catalina Island, where the cast and crew stayed in a residential hotel dominated by elderly patrons who were quite intent on keeping track of their esteemed visitors.

Co-star Bing Crosby recalled that when Carole would come down for breakfast every morning, "all the old ladies would have their ears cocked and their ear-trumpets tuned up waiting to see what she'd say." Lombard found this hilarious and spent her nights dreaming up outrageous comments. One morning she walked in with a flourish, spied Crosby across the crowded room and said loudly, "Oh, Bing? By any chance, did I leave my negligee in your room last night?" (See source no. 038).

Later that same year, during the filming of *Rumba*, Lombard became involved with co-star George Raft, an affair that sparked friendship with Raft's pal and advisor Mack Grey. When Grey entered the hospital suffering from a hernia, Lombard visited him often, and as Grey recalled:

One day I told Carole that *killa* is the Yiddish word for hernia. She thought that was a riot. After Carole heard this, she called me Killer. Carole would walk up to the hospital receptionist and say seriously, "Can I see the Killer?" She had everyone scared of me. They all knew I worked for George Raft and he had this gangster image, and everyone thought I actually was a killer.

Another day, while she was visiting, the doctor came in looking scared. He said, "Are those guards in the hall really necessary?" I didn't know what the hell he's talking about, and I got up and looked in the hall. There were two tough-looking guys holding toy pistols that look real, marching back and forth as if they're protecting my room.

Finally the hospital supervisor showed up. He said to Carole, "We can't have this here in the hospital. What's going on?" The guy almost had a heart attack when she told him, "Look, the mob put out a contract on the Killer's life. He's got to be protected." The supervisor was terrified. "We can't have a shooting in the hospital." But then, by the look on Carole's face, he surmised it's a gag--and we all began to crack up laughing. (See source no. 045).

1935

In the spring of this year Lombard's party spirit had returned following the death of Russ Columbo, and she christened her new Hollywood Boulevard home with a very formal party given along with Bill Powell to celebrate Ronald Colman's return from a stay in England. They called it a black tie affair; black tie in name if not in execution.

Carole detested pretentiousness in Hollywood people, and now that she wasn't married to Powell and didn't have to play up to his hoity-toity friends, she decided to let her hair down and have some laughs.

The theme was *the hospital,* this in response to a string of illnesses suffered by various members of the Hollywood community, and the whole idea was to bring the film world's stuffed shirts back to reality, just this once. Servants dressed in doctor and nurse garb greeted guests, and drinks were served in metal hospital pitchers. Carole seated the crowd around operating tables and presented the food in--*Oh, no!*--bedpans. Bill went along with Carole's gags and smiled weakly as the evening dragged by. It was a memorable night, a kind of a Carole Lombard Strikes Back night. A night that boisterously converted many of Hollywood's social set into Lombard supporters. From here on in, everything she did was larger than life.

That summer Carole and writer Elizabeth Wilson continued their ongoing business of being "friendly enemies." Wilson tried to get an interview and, "Carole told me over the phone that she had a sore throat, her body ached, and she knew it was flu and she probably wouldn't live. So being an old softie and a little upset over losing Carole I sent a huge, and I may add costly, bouquet of white gladiolas and purple hibiscus."

The next Monday, while perusing Louella Parsons' column, Wilson read that Lombard had won an award at a tennis tournament and then celebrated at the Clover Club, all while she supposedly lay on her deathbed. Wilson picked

Lombard and Janet Gaynor at Selznick International during Carole's hectic PR week, July, 1938.

Carole receives a gag gift from Tommy Kelly during a birthday celebration on the Selznick lot, 1937.

up the phone and blistered Lombard's ears, and an hour later a messenger boy arrived with the writer's well-used bouquet of wilted, brown gladiolas and hibiscus. Attached was a note that read, "Take your old flowers--Carole Lombard." According to a speechless Elizabeth Wilson, "I was mortified!" (See source no. 140).

1936

In January, on the night when Lombard was hostessing the Mayfair Ball with its *white* theme, Norma Shearer saw fit to appear in a scarlet gown--the only woman among hundreds to violate Lombard's requested all-white dress code. This episode would later inspire a famous scene in the 1938 Warner Brothers film *Jezebel*, and at the instant that Shearer appeared, David Niven quotes Lombard as saying in a loud voice, "Who the fuck does Norma think she is? The house madam?" (See source no. 025).

Three weeks later a party was given to honor the wife of noted writer Donald Ogden Stewart; it was called *Bea Stewart's Annual Nervous Breakdown Party* because, logically enough, a nervous breakdown had prohibited Mrs. Stewart from attending the Mayfair Ball. Both nighttime travel and large noisy crowds were forbidden for Mrs. Stewart at this time, and her husband invented this "all-white" evening dress party to begin at high noon.

Aside from its unique Nervous Breakdown theme, the affair had the added benefit of being a gag party, with guests asked to brighten the afternoon with any sort of gag that came to mind.

The story is now legend, how a white ambulance screamed up the long driveway of host John Hay Whitney shortly after noon and screeched to a stop at the front door. How the two attendants ran to the back of the ambulance and withdrew, on a stretcher, the lifeless form of Carole Lombard, covered to the neck by a white sheet. How they grimly, urgently raced her inside to the middle of the party and set her down while all around gasped and stood speechless above her. What in the world, they wondered, had happened to their favorite screwball--

"Surprise!" she shrieked happily, sitting up so that the sheet fell away, revealing her White Mayfair gown. More gasps, and hands covered hearts. She sat there as if naked and said, "Don't you get it? This was my gag." She nodded, grinned, imploring them to get it.

It would rank as her most infamous prank, one that drew as much indignation as mirth when it happened, but one that promoted her in the eyes of the press and ultimately nurtured that budding reputation as the preeminent madcap in Hollywood.

1937

Here is a story that typifies Lombard's spirit of *joie de vivre* and her playful streak with stoic Clark Gable. While Hollywood's King was in the service, he recounted this Lombard-Gable encounter to writer A. E. Hotchner: "...He told me about their first duck shoot, early in the morning, the fog too thick to see the ducks, although you could hear them. Carole asked what they could do about it--just sit here in the blind until it clears, Clark told her. She said she had just thought of something they could do while they were waiting--we made love, Clark said, which ain't easy in a duck blind." (See source no. 019).

Carole Lombard was an outspokenly successful businesswoman operating in a town--and world--run by men. "Man thinks he's dealing with an inferior brain when it comes to woman," she said with a sly smile, "and that makes him a sucker." (See source no. 127).

1938

Just before *Made for Each Other* commenced shooting, Selznick International publicity whiz Russell Birdwell, a Lombard crony, came up with the brainstorm of putting Carole in charge of Selznick publicity for an entire week. This eventful seven days began as she appeared at a news desk in front of a large sign that read DANGER -- LOMBARD NOW AT WORK. She raided the prop department for a fire bell that allowed her to call secretaries at will, a .45 caliber pistol with which she took potshots at the ceiling, and a siren, "So David will know I'm here." David Selznick's office was four hundred yards away.

Her promotional device for *Gone With the Wind*, which would begin filming in two short months with--as yet--no Scarlett O'Hara, involved calling Eleanor Roosevelt, the new Duke of Windsor, and George Bernard Shaw to get their opinions on the casting of this vital role. Carole Lombard enjoyed the unlimited use of four phones for five agonizing days, and David Selznick began tearing out his hair when he heard she was calling places like London and Paris.

When things got dull at mid-week, she brought in writer Gene Fowler, one of John Barrymore's gang, to dream up a couple of interesting press releases. Fowler only produced one, as it turned out, but it was a gem of a non sequitur concerning John Hay Whitney, the quiet young financier who was bankrolling Selznick's pre-production of *Gone With the Wind*. The press release went as follows:

In his first interview ever accorded the press, John Hay Whitney yesterday told of his plans for the immediate future.

"I have no immediate future," Mr. Whitney said.

"What are your plans for the past?" he was asked.

"*Gone With the Wind*," he replied, "and you can draw your own conclusions."

Mr. Whitney--or Jock, as he is known to casual acquaintances--sat and stood simultaneously in his offices in Culver City while being interviewed. The interview was arranged by his counsel, Senorita Carole Lombard, the Portugese novelist. Miss Lombard wears a very strong perfume, L'Amour L'Nocturne, designed to keep married executives from making passes at her during business hours.

Mr. Whitney is a rugged alumnus of Yale. He stands well over six million dollars.

"Mr. Whitney," the interviewer asked, after a game warden had got Seniorita Lombard off the ceiling with a butterfly net, "What are your plans for Mr. Selznick's future?"

By sheer guesswork David O. Selznick entered the room at this moment. Mr. Selznick said: "I wish to deny everything Mr. Whitney has said."

Seniorita Lombard explained to Mr. Whitney: "Mr. Selznick is president in charge of production."

"This is news to me," Mr. Whitney said, "Who's going to play Scarlett O'Hara?"

"What race is she in?" countered Selznick.

Mr. Whitney disclosed that this was not only his first interview but also his last.

"What are your plans for Senorita Lombard?" the interviewer asked.

"She's on her own," said Jock. "We're firing her next Tuesday."

On Saturday, July 9, with Lombard's reign on the publicity staff ended, she spent the day acting as Culver City's honorary mayor. Her first official duty was to spread it among the sparse Saturday crew at the studio that the mayor (Carole, in this case) had declared a holiday, and Selznick workers began filing out the gate. By the time the boss showed up to work on *Gone With the Wind,* the sound stages and back lots were completely deserted. Only Carole Lombard could be found, sitting at her news desk, feet up, reading a magazine. Selznick demanded to know where the hell everybody was.

"I gave them the day off," she said matter-of-factly, then added, quoting fellow-mayor Frank Hague of Jersey City, "I *am* the law!" (See sources no. 049 and 115).

Soon thereafter, *Life* writer Noel F. Busch arrived on the scene to work on his feature about Carole, and he sat in on a brainstorming session between Birdwell and Lombard in her bungalow. Of the antic goings-on, Busch said:

> ...In and out whisk Loretta, the maid, who
> has to wash the golden blonde Lombard mop every
> morning so it will always photograph the same
> shade, and Jimmy, the commissary waiter, who
> brings Carole a chicken sandwich and a Coca-Cola
> for her lunch.   It turns out that Jimmy has a
> turkey which he won in a raffle but no place to
> cook it.   "Raffle it again," says Lombard.
> "Great   idea," says Birdwell, "We'll   make
> Selznick buy two tickets. Two dollars apiece."
> "Make it a fake raffle," says Lombard.   "I
> like phony raffles. If it's a phony raffle, I'll
> buy two tickets myself." (See source no. 062).

A month later, in October, Carole signed a new standard contract with the Myron Selznick Talent Agency for
the usual ten percent cut--*except*.   Except that the
contract sent to Lombard wasn't the same one she sent
back.
It struck Carole that it would be terribly funny if
she could trick Myron into signing a contract that gave
Carole ten percent of *his* gross, instead of the other way
around.   Nobody read the fine print on contracts if they
could avoid it, and Carole figured that hard-living Myron
in particular wouldn't read it, so she took the contract
to a printer, had almost exact replicas made, sent them
back for Myron's signature, and lo and behold, there in
the mail came a contract bearing Myron Selznick's autograph. All legal, all very funny. Wow, the money she
could rake in now!
She let it slip matter-of-factly one day to Myron
that she wanted her ten percent of *his* ten percent of the
hundred grand he had secured for Fredric March in a recent
deal and Myron naturally stared at her blankly. "Why you
son of a bitch!" she railed.   "You welcher! Don't you
play dumb with me."
She showed him the cold, hard facts in black and
white, and Myron Selznick nearly cried.
Later, the pair would part somewhat acrimoniously,
but until his death in 1944, Myron would brag about what
Lombard had done to him, and he framed that contract and
hung it in his office. (See source no. 036).

1939

In mid-production of *Vigil in the Night,* director
George Stevens mentioned to Carole that he was about to
spend the weekend duck hunting, since the season had arrived, and she in turn mentioned how Pa was itching to go,
so naturally she invited Stevens to go with them. Stevens
wanted to know where they would be going, and Carole explained that Harry Fleischmann's duck club in Bakersfield

was the preferred spot.

"Uh-uh," said Stevens, "the best duck hunting is in Imperial Valley around Salton Sea."

"Bakersfield," said Lombard.

"Imperial," said Stevens.

They went their separate ways at six o'clock on Friday evening, and Carole proceeded to spend the entire weekend planning, from the duck blinds of Bakersfield, her Monday morning gag. On Sunday she put in a call to the Imperial Valley. As she had hoped, the duck hunting there was lousy. She arrived at RKO early on Monday morning and went to work, giggling all the while. When George Stevens arrived at his office, he found dead ducks hanging from light fixtures and furniture. A half dozen live ducks quacked from a metal cage on the floor. A decoy stared blankly from the middle of his desk, and leaning against it was a card that read, "Personally, we didn't have any trouble finding ducks. So, how many did you get?"

1941

Before coming to America from England, director Alfred Hitchcock had issued his famous proclamation to the effect that actors are nothing but cattle to be herded about. Lombard knew of Hitchcock's genius and convinced him to sign for the film *Mr. and Mrs. Smith*, and was well prepared for her razzing of the new guy on the block. According to Hitchcock: "...when I arrived on the set, the first day of shooting, Carole Lombard had had a corral built, with three sections, and in each one there was a live young cow. Round the neck of each of them there was a white disk tied on with a ribbon, with three names: Carole Lombard, Robert Montgomery, and the name of a third member of the cast, Gene Raymond." (See source no. 040). Hitchcock appreciated the Lombard sense of humor, calling it "spectacular repartee," and they became such fast friends that he and his wife were soon leasing Carole's old house on St. Cloud Road in Bel Air.

EVERY ACTOR SHOULD TAKE AT LEAST ONE WEEK'S WHIRL AT PUBLICITY by Carole Lombard

Publicity is one of the most important--if not the most important topic--under discussion in Hollywood today. The motion picture capital has come to a long overdue realization that its publicity, foremost among its contacts with the rest of the world, has the power to make Hollywood the most beloved place on earth or the most hated. That, of course, goes for all the personalities in Hollywood.

A lot of us have wondered what makes a publicity office tick and what goes on behind the scenes where the big sales ideas are born and developed. I've had many contacts with film press agents while working in pictures but only when I spent a week as a working publicist at Selznick International was I able to see the wheels go 'round.

It was a six-day, full-time job. I worked every minute of it. Fun? Never had a better time in my life. There's more romance in the everyday work of a publicity office than in the work of any other single department on a movie lot. And you can take that straight--without a chaser.

The fun, of course, is merely incidental. Any star knows, or should know, the importance of publicity. This is not exactly a recital of what I learned in a week at Selznick-International's praisery, for you cannot learn much about publicity in that time. It has always been a prideful point with me that I have taken a personal and necessary interest in publicity, and believe I have come to know as much about it as any other person who has not made that branch of journalism a life career.

It is in the publicity offices of Hollywood's motion picture studios that careers have been made--and cracked. Here, every day of the week, are men and women who have in their hands millions of dollars' worth of careers. Theirs is the work of creating interest in players and pictures, jumping the value of an actor with every well-timed line of news or chatter. And at the same moment theirs is the power to blot a career with an ill-chosen idea that can ruin years of effort. Is it any wonder that stars must make it their business to know publicity from the ground up?

The business of putting all other interests aside for a week and doing publicity work myself, with my own hands, so to speak, was a new experience for me. Now that it's over, I can say with complete conviction that all film players should try it. The idea that publicity consists simply of writing pieces for the papers has gone to the same limbo where silent pictures now roost.

In the first place, publicity is not a pursuit dedicated to the grabbing of all the free space the traffic will bear. Publicity, I learned, is journalism, plus salesmanship, plus diplomacy, plus showmanship. In the second place, the space itself does not mean a thing. In

the third place, it is far better to never get one's name
in the paper than to have whole columns which say the
wrong thing.

The entire workings of a well-ordered publicity department will teach one that every effort, even down to
the smallest, is or should be directed among pre-conceived
lines, with all of these dove-tailing into a definite
sales campaign.

What features of a picture are to be sold heaviest?
What angle will best convince the public the picture must
be seen? How are the personalities in the cast to be
handled? What is the best way to present them to the public, considering the type of roles they are playing?
These are but a few of the basic questions you will hear
around the office...

A common charge leveled against press agentry in
general is that it lives on a diet of hokum. That may be
true in too many quarters today, but it doesn't hold among
those who have kept pace with the technical improvements
in other branches of the film industry. Hokum, one may
learn in a publicity office, is as outmoded as the spin-
ning wheel. Not only outmoded, but also outworn, ineffec-
tive and downright dangerous.

Your modern press agent believes that hokum is the
resort of publicity men too lazy to dig for something
truthful, which nine times out of ten makes a better story
anyway. Remember, too, that the unseen welcome mat before
the editor's door is not nailed down, and may be hauled
out on short notice. There's a string attached to it for
the man that tries to "put one across" the second time.

That leads us to another subject, which can be called
the "developing of news." One of the quickest-learned
(and most deflating) truths around the publicity office is
that city editors do not swoon at the sound of the names
that glitter in lights. Names that come popping at city
editors every week cease to be news in themselves, unless
there is news attached to them. That is why "developing
of news" is important.

In using this procedure, your publicist goes out and
makes news happen. He gets his idea first, then executes
it. When completed, the idea makes a story. It's all
true enough, in the final analysis, because it *did* happen,
and it has to possess the kind of newsworthy merit that
practically cries out for printing.

We hatched a couple of such ideas...during my hectic
week. One was for a round-the-world telephone poll of
notables, getting their views on who should play Scarlett
O'Hara in *Gone With the Wind*. The Duke of Windsor and
George Bernard Shaw were a couple of the names on our
list. Another was in connection with *Titanic,* and included the dropping of a wreath by the first Pan-American
trans-Atlantic Clipper plane over the spot where the
Titanic sank, the flowers bearing the legend "To those who
showed the way to safety on the high seas."

The true test of publicity is not how much is said,

but what is said, whether in a newspaper, a magazine, over the air or by word of mouth.   President Roosevelt performed one of the best press agent services in months when, during the Birthday Ball in Washington, he called Janet Gaynor "cute as a button." Just four words there, but how well he described our good friend, and how the newspapers and magazines snapped it up.

In my opinion, the time is coming when the field of publicity will have reached such heights that it well may be the toughest branch in the business to break into.   I wonder how many people in Hollywood realize there are more than 400 correspondents of one kind and another in town, every one feeding the world Hollywood news.   Each individual style, a special preference in news, a different audience for his material.   A press agent has to satisfy these markets and write for them.

Every star in Hollywood ought to take the time to work a week in a publicity department.   They would find six full days of surprises and, I might mention, hard work.

Besides, they would hear from the press itself what it wants and why, without any triple-play relays in between.

Try it yourself some time.

[Copyright *The Hollywood Reporter,* 18th Anniversary Issue. Originally run on October 24, 1938.]

WHY IS CAROLE LOMBARD HIDING OUT FROM HOLLYWOOD?
by Frederick McFee for *Screen Book,* October, 1938

Hollywood's greatest paradox of the moment is one that has the entire film city wondering.

And you'd wonder, too, if one of the favorite daughters of *your* town, without any warning, suddenly decided to get away--oh, far away--from It All. That's what happened when Carole Lombard, who has long been synonymous with good fellowship and popularity, decided to go into the Great Silence.

Popular night spots of the film town no longer ring with the beautiful lady's hearty laughter (and that's a great loss, because that guffaw of Carole's can do more to instill happiness than anything else I know of!). Reporters, once Carole's boon companions, are greeted with politeness if not cordiality (for over a year she has refused to give interviews--even on the most abstract of subjects).

Of course there have been a lot of rumors about Carole's sudden and voluntary retirement from public life. Some of them have been unkind--some tempered with tolerance. But all rumors come back to the same moot point-- why is Carole absenting herself from the Hollywood scene?

Carole's romance with Clark Gable is perhaps one of the most publicized in the world today. The gossips have it that Mr. G. himself is responsible for Carole's "I won't talk" attitude. They hint darkly at dissention between the present Mrs. Gable and her spouse that prevents the usual divorce and the expected happy ending of the Carole-Clark romance. But whether it's true or not, Hollywood resents the fact that the happy-go-lucky Lombard that it once knew is no longer part of its colorful present.

You see, Hollywood knows the girl as she really is--a big-hearted, cheerful gal who began her career over a decade ago as a Mack Sennett bathing beauty. On the screen, she may put across the idea that she is a giddy, pertly irresponsible, always-wisecracking blonde. Off the screen, she has a famous--and volcanic--vocabulary; but in a town where selfishness is a synonym for self-preservation, she goes out of her way to do things for people. Gratis--impulsively--instinctively.

You have had inklings, perhaps, of the Lombard big-heartedness. So have I. They led me to look for definite evidence. And the evidence accumulated not only makes a case. It makes an untold story.

This doing-things-for-people isn't a new facet of the Lombard personality, like her recent elusiveness toward the Press. She simply has never talked about anything she has ever done for anybody. She couldn't be bludgeoned into confessing. But if you know people close to her, and can get them to talk (you have to promise not to mention their names), you hear some amazing things about Carole. Things that have been going on for years--ever since she was a bathing girl.

That's how she started in this movie game, as a kid in her early teens. Most people know that. But what they don't know is this:

One of her pals on that old Sennett lot was another bathing girl, named Madalynne Fields. As insiders tell the tale today, Carole's option was picked up and Madalynne's wasn't. Perhaps Madalynne would have connected somewhere else; perhaps not. But Carole wasn't going to let down her best pal....

They were together until recently, when Madalynne became the wife of that fine movie director, Walter Lang. But as "Fieldsie," Carole's pal became a Hollywood legend. Anyone who knows Carole knows that she seldom moved without consulting her secretary friend. And the steady sureness of Carole's rise, and the extent of her success, made the shrewd observers suspect that Fieldsie is one of the smartest girls in Hollywood.

Carole would deny heatedly that she has ever done anything for Fieldsie. She would insist that she hasn't done Fieldsie any favor, having her around. Fieldsie had done her the favor, *staying* around.

Her habit of befriending people has paid her dividends like these only this once. But Carole never has thought of that angle. She wouldn't.

There was what she did for Margaret Tallichet, for example. Margaret had come to Hollywood to try to get in the movies, had had no luck, and determined to stay close to them, if not in them, had got a job as a stenographer at Paramount. She landed in the publicity department.

The legend has it that Carole first saw her there. That isn't true. One day an interviewer (this was back in the good old pre-elusive days!) had an appointment with Carole. Margaret's boss, who was busy, sent Margaret to sit in on the interview. Carole said afterward, "I couldn't talk. I couldn't keep my eyes off that girl."

She found out the girl's name. The next day, she walked into the surprised secretary's office and took her off to meet Adolph Zukor, head of the studio. Without any ballyhoo (Carole was against it), Margaret was enrolled in the studio's acting school. Two months later, she was given a test. Nothing came of it. One broken-hearted girl saw herself going back to a typewriter for keeps. Carole saw something else.

She persuaded Zeppo Marx, a friend and an agent, to make an exception just once and have an unknown for a client. He interested Producer David O. Selznick in testing Margaret. Weeks passed afterward, with no word. Carole, herself, talked Selznick into making an elaborate second test.

To get "the right clothes," for Margaret, Carole raided the Paramount wardrobe department. That appealed to her sense of humor. Wouldn't it be ironic for one studio, which hadn't been interested, to help another to find a new star?   She also bought clothes for Margaret. She talked to her by the hour, and had Clark Gable do likewise, giving her tips. Margaret was signed after that second test, given a "bit" in *A Star Is Born*, then sent East by Selznick for a year's training in little theatres and a year's study of glamor, poise, and everything else a star should have.   Margaret Tallichet is in for a big build-up--and all because of Carole!

Then, there is Alice Marble.   Carole tried to talk her into a screen career.   Alice, whose greatest ambition was to be the foremost net star of the country, couldn't be interested. She's still striving. If she *does* attain her ambition, then perhaps there'll be time for a movie career--and Carole may attain her frustrated ambition to see Alice Marble on the screen!

Ambitions like that aren't usual in Hollywood.   Far from it.   Few stars ever go out of their way to help, or even encourage, girls who *might* develop into screen rivals.   Self-preservation argues against it.   But does Carole think of that angle? The evidence says: "No."

Three years ago, a picture crew was flying East for location work when their plane crashed. Some were killed. One electrician almost died, was in a hospital for months, finally recovered with a leg amputated.   Under workmen's compensation, the studio had to pay his medical expenses. But the studio went farther--it promised him that when he was able to get about again, he could have his job back. He learned how to walk with an artificial leg.   Then, somehow, no one seemed to remember the promise of work. Carole heard about it.   She saw red.   She had one of her impulses.

At that time, she and the studio were in the throes of contract talk.   She went to the Front Office and said, "I want that man kept on the payroll, given work.   I won't sign, if he isn't." The studio said that it was an oversight that he hadn't been re-hired, and put him back to work.

A couple of days later, a radio gossiper broadcast the story--and the studio told the electrician, "You're through."   Even though Carole publicly denied the story. He was idle four or five months.   Now, by saying nothing, doing nothing to add fuel to the fire, he finally has his job back.   But, as the studio executive who told me this inside story (in whispers) pointed out: if Carole had signed that contract, she would have seen to it that that electrician never was fired, no matter what happened. But she decided to become a free-lance, instead.   She had no weapon with which to continue the fight.

P. S.   She didn't know the electrician, except by sight.

She's the same way, if anyone she knows is sick. She doesn't take the simple, easy way of remembering.   She doesn't just call up her florist and have him send around a basket of flowers and consider her duty done.   She'll

send flowers, yes.   But she will also rack her brain   to
think of some present that will be really useful,   something that will last.

Travis Banton, the designer of all of Carole's
clothes, can tell you.   When he was in the hospital not so
long ago, she took the trouble to find out what was   the
most annoying thing about his slow convalescence.   It was
the fact that he couldn't seem to get warm.   She sent him
a blanket.

There   was   a hairdresser (not Carole's own) who   was
struck in the eye in an accident.   Her eyeball was   punc-
tured.   Carole heard about it.   Whether or not she helped
with the hospital bills, no one will ever know.   But   I
happen to know that she can be suspected of it.   I know of
her   taking time out to think of what might be useful   to
that blinded girl, in that hospital bed.   She went down-
town, herself, to get a bed jacket for her.

When   someone is sick,   she doesn't   content   herself
with one thoughtful gift.   She spends hours,   thinking of
gag presents--things to make even invalids laugh.   Dr.
Lombard believes in the medicine of laughter.

Everybody knows Carole's love for animals.   Everybody
knows,   also,   that her favorite pet of all time was   her
dog, Pushface, which played in *Love Before Breakfast,* and
in whose behalf Carole at the time took out full-page   ads
in the local trade papers.   But few people know what has
happened to Pushface.

"Push," as she called him, was very fond of her maid.
The maid was crazy about the dog.   So what should   Carole
do but give Pushface to the maid--who is the "day" variety
and lives "outside." It wasn't easy to part with Pushface.
But   giving him to the maid appealed to her as a   way   to
make   both the dog and the girl happy.   That's typical of
her.

Any   interviewer   who has ever talked to Carole   for
five   minutes   about her career has   heard her   say,   "In
Twentieth Century, in six weeks, I learned more   about
acting from John Barrymore than I've learned   from   other
people in all the years I've been in films." She   isn't
afraid to acknowledge her debts.   And she has a   long
memory.

A few months ago, John Barrymore was let out by MGM.
He went over to Paramount, doing a series of *Bulldog Drum-
mond* pictures.   Everybody felt   sorry   for   "America's
greatest actor," reduced now to featured billing--in B
pictures.   Everybody, that is, but Carole.   To her, he
wasn't through.   All he needed was a chance.

She saw a spot for him in *True Confession*.   It wasn't
a typical Barrymore role.   All the better.   It would prove
how much acting he still had in his system.   She saw to it
that he was given the role.   Result: every other one of
the   comment cards from the sneak preview mentioned
Barrymore.   He all but stole the picture!   And Carole is
tickled silly.   It's A pictures for John from now on!

You won't get Carole to admit that she had any hand
in his getting the role. You won't get the Front Office
to admit it.   But let me point out that he wouldn't have
been in the picture if Carole hadn't wanted him there.
She has a voice in the casting of her pictures.

At Paramount, making a strong comeback, is Evelyn
Brent--who was a star when Carole still was pretty much an
unknown.   She has had some good roles recently, but she
could do with some better ones. Carole saw a spot for her
in *True Confession*.   She promoted Evelyn for the role.
Director Wesley Ruggles argued for another girl.   He finally won--for reasons that don't need detailing here.
The important point is: Carole Lombard tried to give
Evelyn Brent a break.

Few stars go in for impulses like that.   Most stars,
if they ever think of one-time stars trying for comebacks,
think, "They've had their day. Why don't they give up?"

Carole, you see, can put herself in the other
fellow's place.   It's an uncommon talent, in this every-
body-for-himself town.

She learned that her stand-in for a recent picture--a
new girl--was planning to be married during the picture.
Twice the wedding had to be postponed, because of the
picture schedule.   The girl set a third date. For a Saturday night.   Director Ruggles, early that afternoon,
decided to have the company work that night.   About 5:30,
Carole suddenly--and very conveniently--fell ill, couldn't
go on working. Her stand-in had her wedding.

Two other incidents, typical of Carole, happened on
this set.

There was a bit player, a man, who had one line to
deliver.   On take after take, he muffed it. Ruggles was
really a paragon of patience.   He saw about six takes
spoiled. Finally, he said he was going to get someone
else for that "bit." Carole took Ruggles off to one side
and persuaded him to keep this player, give him six more
tries, if necessary.

Few stars would have done that.   Most of them would
have blown up after the second take, *demanding* a replacement. I know: I've seen it happen. But Carole knew
what the loss of that bit would do to that man.   Even bit
players' reputations get bruised around Hollywood.   He
would have found it hard to get another job.   Carole
thought of that angle. Carole would.

Then, there was the day that two of her leading men
had a difficult scene together, with Carole sitting on the
sidelines.   Time after time, they tried it.   Time after
time, something happened to spoil the take.   Finally, it
looked as if they had it when--somebody coughed. A prop
man, somewhere behind Carole.

Ruggles whirled around, with fire in his eye.
Somebody was going to get a verbal blistering.   Maybe
somebody was going to lose his job.   Maybe somebody was
going to be murdered!

Carole spoke up, to say: "I'm awfully sorry, Wes. I

couldn't help it. I couldn't old it any longer."
    There have been rumors of late that Carole is begin-
ning to come out of her shell. As a publicity gag for her
new David O. Selznick picture, *Made for Each Other,* she
became head of the publicity department, and had herself a
grand time planting yarns with all the leading columnists
and writers.   According to rumor, she was all set to call
up such varied personalities as Mrs. Roosevelt, the Duke
of Windsor and George Bernard Shaw to find out what they
thought of the casting of *Gone With the Wind* (also a
Selznick production) until forcibly called off.   When, for
another publicity stunt, she was made mayor of Culver
City, Carole promptly called a public holiday for all
studio employees. Selznick tried to remonstrate with her,
whereupon the original Miss Lombard, emulating that famous
Eastern mayor, said forcibly, "I am the law!" (And she
got away with it!)
    That would indicate that eventually Hollywood will
soon see the return of the laughing Carole that it used to
know.
    Maybe she's learned that she shouldn't hide away from
the town that loves her!

LOMBARD--AS SHE SEES HERSELF by Gladys Hall for *Motion Picture*, November, 1938

I had a date to interview Carole, at one o'clock sharp, in her dressing-room bungalow on the Selznick lot where she and Jimmy Stewart are making *Made for Each Other*. The picture in which, for the first time in two years, Carole gives up comedy antics and turns serious, even dramatic; the part of a woman who, when she laughs, laughs through tears. (Are you wondering which comes easier to Carole, to laugh or to cry...to be grave or gay?...)

Suddenly, from without, just on the stroke of one, came the crind of car wheels, war whoops, symbals of loud laughter and as at a summons, a stimulant, heads raised and voices shouted, "That's Lombard!" And Lombard it was, to be sure. On time to the minute, as I said. Undaunted by the heat of an "unseasonable" California day. Constitutionally undaunted by anything. That's Lombard, too.

Yes, indeed, Lombard arriving in her two-year-old Ford coupe, the only car she owns and driving it herself, as usual. Laughing about it later when I said to her, "No foolin', is it *really* the only car you own? What about when you and Clark go to premieres, to the Troc, to dinner parties at houses encircled with limousines as long as the *Queen Mary* and other glittering, chauffeur-driven equipages?"...and Carole said, "*When* we go to premieres, et cetera, we go in my Ford. What's the matter with it? Gets us there, doesn't it?"

So there was Lombard, having a day off, wearing firemen red *crepe de chine* slacks, a careless beige pullover, careless pale hair, windrough; no make-up. No make-up coating her lively mind, either. No make-up artificing her fearless, life-loving spirit.

Carole is a provocative figure. Carole and Bette Davis are the only two women I have ever met who house vigorous, brutally frank minds in bodies as feminine as filigree and fine lace. Carole evokes imaginings of many kinds. But it would be totally impossible for the most vivid imagination to imagine her saying anything she doesn't mean, doing anything posey or phony. Carole has never learned to assume a false front, never has learned to conceal her likings or dislikings. And her sound instinct has taught her that to be a human being, without hokum, without affectations is a far, far better thing than to be a Prima Donna wearing a false face that deceives no one.

Carole stares life smack in the face and laughs. Slender as a willow sapling, made with the fine-boned delicacy of a *Sevres* figurine, fragile lines and white skin and, seemingly, breakable to the touch, Lombard is as healthy-hearted as a peasant, as sturdy-spirited as the rich earth because, like a peasant, she stands rooted in realities, is at home with realities and a stranger to sham.

Lombard gives Gable an impish grin while posing for photographs at the Encino ranch, 1939.

We walked over to her bungalow, Carole and I. At least, I walked. Carole got there by executing a few spirals and curves and a leap upon her scooter-bike which stands in front of her bungalow handy for her excursions around the lot. Lombard-wise, her fellow workers in the studios think nothing of seeing Lombard streak by them upon her scooter-bike, wearing a pair of slacks or a formal so exquisite and perishable that you would think it would be--ah, Mr. Selznick--gone with the wind...She is "almost forever" laughing, is Carole. She is like something wound up at high tension. But as high tension is her natural *metier* it *is* natural.

In the bungalow Carole dunked her very slim length in a chair, legs over the arm, ran her hands through her hair, ordered iced coffee and sandwiches for the two of us. And said that she had been skeet-shooting, that she is "nuts about skeet-shooting," that skeet-shooting "gets you," that you keep saying "just one more round" and keep ON saying it until old Sol has run round the clock, likely as not. She didn't say that she had been skeet-shooting with Clark. And maybe she hadn't. But Clark has often told me that he spends a good part of his between-the-scenes time skeet-shooting. And so I became a master mathematician and put two and two together and it totaled up to Carole and Clark skeet-shooting the morning away and what of it.

Carole continued her rave about skeet-shooting and wound up saying "--but it's the same with everything I do. I *love* everything I do. I'm intensely interested in and enthusiastic about everything I do, *everything*. No matter what it is I'm doing, no matter how trivial, it isn't trivial to me. I give it all I got and I love it. I love living, I love life. Eating, sleeping, waking up again, skeet-shooting, sitting around an old barn doing nothing, my work, taking a bath, talking my ears off, the little things, the big things, the simplest things, the most complicated things--I get a kick out of everything I do while I'm doing it.

"If I don't love what I'm doing I don't DO it. But if I have to do something I'm not nuts about now and then, as who doesn't, I DO it and get it over with. I never anticipate trouble. I never worry, never fret. I can't duck issues. Ducking issues causes more grief than the issues themselves ever do. I never sit around and clutch my head and moan 'I HAVE to do so-and-so, alas Lo, the poor Lombard!'--I just say 'Let's DO it' or 'Okay, let's GO!'--and it's done and there's nothing to it."

I considered Carole, lopping there in her chair, throwing her arms wide open to life, knowing it to be good, exulting in it...and I thought back to the time, not so long ago, when Hollywood called her its "Play Girl," its "Good Scout"; when Lombard stood upon the Midway and Lombard and a laugh were synonymous, one and the same thing. And still are. Though the Play Girl plays, now, within a more restricted circle of friends and the Good Scout is no longer pranking on the Midway where all who run may see.

The truth about Lombard is that she takes the serious things in life seriously, the light things lightly, laughs at a joke, weeps at a sorrow, enormously loves the whole of it, as a mother loves a child, its faults as well as its virtues, its tantrums and its talents.

There is no better craftswoman in all Hollywood than Lombard. Nor any star who takes her work more seriously, is more painstakingly familiar with the tools of her trade. If you have an idea that Lombard larrups through a picture, how wrong you are! No guesswork, this, for I've heard it from every director, cameraman, actor, actress or extra who has ever worked with her. She studies a script until the ink is absorbed right off the page. She knows good writing. She has a critical faculty second to none when it comes to detecting weaknesses or appreciating strength and fine characterization in a script. She knows her own part inside out before she steps foot on a sound stage. And she knows everything there is to be known about everybody else's parts, too. When she is working she is on the set at nine o'clock sharp. She knows her lines. She knows her business. She has made it her business to know it.

"I love my work and I take it seriously," Lombard told me...and when I said to her: "How about playing this dramatic part in *Made for Each Other?* Do you like it or would you rather continue to play film flitterbugs like Irene in *My Man Godfrey,* the loony lady in *Nothing Sacred* and others? Which comes easier to you?"

She said, "They're not really so different. You know the old thing, comedy and tragedy are akin? Like lots of old things, it's the truth. Back of all comedy there is tragedy; back of every good belly-laugh there is a familiarity with things not funny at all. There must be. *You* laugh with tears in your eyes, don't you?" demanded Lombard, "most of us do. And Irene in *Godfrey* was, I'd say, the most difficult part I ever played. Because Irene was a complicated and, believe it or not, essentially a tragic person...."

When Carole said, "Back of every good belly-laugh there is a familiarity with things not funny at all," I knew that she could well be speaking of herself, of her own childhood, of the first seven years of her life which might well have blunted a less shining spirit, years when her father was so dangerously ill that Carole and her mother lived in a constant strain; years when Carole and her mother lived in small, ground-floor flats, strangers to the over-privileges of Hollywood stars. And when I spoke to Carole of her early childhood and what it might have done to her she laughed and said: "Being poor didn't matter a bit. *I* didn't mind a bit. Wouldn't mind living in a ground-floor flat right now--you can get out the back door faster!"

Then we both laughed. Because it wasn't funny and we both knew it wasn't funny. And that's Lombard, too....

"I had a lot of fun doing the screwy comedies," Carole went on, "but I was getting pretty tired of them. Hollywood has done too many of them. The old 'sheep' angle, you know. Now, I'd like to do two dramatic pictures, then another comedy and so vary the ingredients a bit.

"Yep," said Carole, "I love my work and I take it seriously. As I love everything I do and give everything I've got to whatever I'm doing. But I do not go about clutching my Career to an otherwise naked bosom. If my work were to be taken away from me tomorrow I wouldn't be stopped. I'd go on living, and still love it. There are a thousand things I could do, would do, would want to do. I'm like old Solomon. If he'd lost one of his wives he wouldn't exactly have been a widower. I couldn't be widowed by the loss of any one facet of my life. Because it's too rich, life is too abundant. There are too many things to want to do, to have, to get, to lose, to find out about...."

I said, "You know yourself pretty well, don't you?"

"Good person to get acquainted with, yourself," laughed Carole.

I said, perceiving that Lombard was running true to form and making a game of the interview, having fun doing it in spite of hell and high water and the fact that she doesn't especially like to give interviews...I said, "Okay, what's your worst fault, then? Riddle me that one."

"Too much energy," said Carole promptly.

"Your best trait next?"

"My disposition. It's *veddy* good. I was born that way. I'm always happy. I never get mad at little things, trifles. It takes a *terrific* thing to make me mad. Then, when the terrific thing gets me I do a beautiful job of it."

I said, "Are you temperamental? You know, walk off sets and things?"

"No-yes, a hyphenated answer," said Carole. "I do walk off sets but not for the reasons you might suppose. I'm not temperamental about myself. I can take care of myself, all right. But I do get temperamental when I hear some little would-be Napoleon of a director, some little killer-diller of a petty czar cursing out extras, grips, electricians. I've walked off sets when things like that happen. And will again, if and when they happen again. I've said to the pettifogging Nappies, 'Why don't you bawl me out if that's the way you feel about it? You don't dare to bawl the stars out, do you? They could bark right back at you, couldn't they? So you have to light on the little fellows, the ones who can't talk back, don't you?' It's an obsession with me," said Carole, savagely, "the

bullying of men who can't defend themselves by men who,
not necessarily stronger, are in stronger positions. I've
tweaked more than one nose, twisted more than one ear
until it *rasssppped* for that sort of thing."

"Any other pet hates?" I quizzed, professorially,
"like lizards, you know, or pencils scratching on black-
boards?"

"Affectations," said Lombard. "I can't STAND affected people--or snobs. And I don't stand them. I do something *horrible* to them to break them down. I hate to be
yessed, too. If someone doesn't like me in a picture, for
instance, I don't want them to *purr* over me, I want them
to TELL me so."

I said, "Do you take people on faith or are you apt
to be cynical about them?"

"On faith," said Carole, "then, if they prove to be
wrong, I'm through."

"Any fear of anything? Old age, for instance...?"

"I don't like height," said Carole, laboring visibly
to dig up a sizable fear for me. "I fly, I don't mind
that. But I can't stand on high buildings or high places
and look down. Apart from that, no. There is nothing I
am afraid of. Least of all, old age. I NEVER want to be
Sixteen again. I think that eighteen is the DULLEST age
in the world. If ever I was unhappy, it was when I was in
my teens. That's because you don't understand anything
when you're that young. You're puzzled and so you're
hurt. For only the things you don't understand have the
power to hurt you, like the Power of Darkness. With age
there comes a richness that's *divine*. Age takes on a
beauty everyone can't see, perhaps. But I see it...I
don't know of anything in the world *more* beautiful, more
fascinating than a woman ripe with years, rich and lush as
velvet with experience, her humor as tangy and flavorous
as sunriped fruit. If women wouldn't get so *self-
conscious* about getting old they wouldn't get old mentally
and then they wouldn't *be* old at all, only wise and simply
divine. I LOVE the idea of getting old," said Lombard,
thus loving one aspect of life which is nightmare to nine
women out of every ten and The Bugaboo, certainly, to
every celebrated Beauty.

"Clothes...shopping...how much part do clothes play
in your life?"

"So-so," said Carole, "clothes don't stimulate me
very much. I buy good things but not a great many things.
Two or three outfits a season and let it go at that. I
like sports things, sweaters and slacks and suits...

"I save my dough, I'm no fool," grinned Carole. "The
terribly important thing to me is a home. I have a lot of
fun out of having a home. And I know exactly the kind of
a house I'm going to build one of these days, probably in
the San Fernando Valley. It will be very small but every
detail will be exactly as I want it. I'm not the type to
say it's my Dream House," laughed Carole, "but IT IS!"

Carole was having fun when she said "I save my dough, I'm no fool." But, matter of fact, it was one of those many-a-true-word-spoken-in-jest things. For Carole is one of the few who doesn't figure her income in terms of what you may read she gets paid for a picture. She figures her earnings in terms of *what she has left over* after she has deducted her income tax, her living expenses, the amount she sets aside and labels "Savings." She is an excellent business woman, La Lombard. You can mark that down on her slate. She knows exactly how much she earns, exactly the numerals she must put on her check for income tax, exactly how much she must "set aside." She says, "I get 13 cents on the dollar and I know it. So I don't figure that I've earned a dollar, I figure that I've earned 13 cents. And that is all right with me, too. We still don't starve in the picture business after we've divided with the Government. Taxes go to build schools, to maintain the public utilities we all use, so why not? But I live accordingly, that's all. I've had girls show me diamond bracelets, say, "I bought this little thing the other day, such a bargain, only $20,000!' If I bought a little trinket for $20,000--and I never have yet--I'd say, 'There goes my profit for the year, in a hunk of diamond!' It's my disposition again," said Carole happily, "I was born without costly cravings!" (There was not, I may add, a jewel to be seen upon Miss Lombard.)

"I run my house economically. I live comfortably. I loathe the miser in man or mouse. Detest skimpers and hoarders. I just don't cut paper-dolls out of greenbacks, that's all. I use my head before I whip out the check-book...I've got one extravagance--giving people things. It's a form of self-indulgence. I get more out of the giving than the recipients do out of the getting, no doubt.

I said, as Lombard laughed again, "Are you always happy? I mean, don't you ever get low in your mind, feel depressed?"

"Not for more than five minutes at a time," said Lombard. "I'm very seldom depressed. Never morbid. I wouldn't let it get that far. And the only time I'm depressed is when I'm bored. And when I'm bored it's always with myself, no one and nothing else. And when I get bored with myself, find myself uninteresting, it's because my vitality is in low key. And when that happens I just strap on a sandal and DO something about it. I never sit and brood.

"The whole thing is," said Carole, "I never say 'I HAVE to do it,' I say 'Let's get it done!' I believe, too, that we bring to the screen the same qualities we bring to living..."

And Carole brings to the screen positiveness, directness, a great enthusiasm for living.

And God pity liars, snobs, poseurs, phonies, poor-mouths from coming under the scrutiny of the Lombard lens!

REPORT OF THE CIVIL AERONAUTICS BOARD

Of the investigation of an accident involving aircraft of
United States registry NC 1946 which occurred near Las
Vegas, Nevada, on January 16, 1942. File no. 119-42.
Docket No. SA-58. Adopted: July 16, 1942. Released:
July 20, 1942.

1. Conduct of Investigation

An accident involving aircraft NC 1946 occurred in
the vicinity of Las Vegas, Nevada, on January 16, 1942,
about 7:20 p.m. (PST). The aircraft was being operated at
the time in scheduled air carrier service between New
York, New York, and Los Angeles, California, as Flight 3
of Transcontinental and Western Air, Inc., (hereinafter
referred to as "TWA"). The accident resulted in fatal injuries to all of the 19 passengers and the crew of three
and in destruction of the airplane.

The Washington office of the Civil Aeronautics Board
(hereinafter reffered to as the "Board") received notice
of the accident about 11:15 p.m. The Board immediately
initiated an investigation in accordance with the provisions of Section 702(a)(2) of the Civil Aeronautics Act of
1938, as amended (hereinafter referred to as the "Act").
An Air Safety Investigator of the Board arrived at Las
Vegas, Nevada, about 1:30 a.m., January 18, 1942, and immediately proceeded to the scene of the accident.[1] In the
meantime, searching parties, including United States Army
personnel and Deputy Sheriffs of Clark County, Nevada,
commenced a search for the airplane. Because of the inac-
cessibility of the point at which the accident occurred,
the wreckage was not reached until about 9:00 o'clock on
the morning following the accident. The wreckage was
placed under guard by deputy sheriffs until the following
morning when a military guard was established. This guard
was maintained until the wreckage was officially released
to the company on January 31, 1942.

A public hearing was held at Los Angeles, California,
on January 23 and 24, 1942. Robert W. Chrisp, an attorney
for the Board, acting as presiding examiner, and the following personnel of the Safety Bureau of the Board parti-
cipated in the hearing: R. D. Hoyt, Assistant Director;
Frank E. Caldwell, Chief, Investigation Division; and
Warren E. Carey, Senior Air Safety Investigator.

Since 15 members of the United States Army Air Corps
were passengers on the airplane, the Board invited the Air
Corps to participate in the investigation of the accident.
Major George W. Haskins attended the proceedings as repre-
sentative of the Air Corps.

All the evidence available to the Board at the time
was presented at the hearing. Testimony was given by 12
witnesses, including experts in various technical subjects
involved in the investigation, and 17 exhibits were re-

ceived in evidence.   Depositions of other witnesses were
taken and have been made a part of the record.   While the
examiner and other representatives of the Board and the
Air Corps were the only ones designated to asks questions
directly of the witnesses, the examiner, acting under in-
structions of the board, announced at the opening of the
hearing that any person who had any evidence, questions,
or suggestions to present for consideration in the proceedings might submit them in writing to the examiner.
Nineteen questions were submitted and were asked of the
appropriate witnesses.
     Upon the basis of all the evidence disclosed by the
investigation, the Board now makes its report in accordance with the provisions of the Act.

     II. Summary and analysis of evidence.

     Air Carrier: At the time of the accident, TWA was an
air carrier operating under currently effective certificates of public convenience and necessity and air carrier
operating certificates.   These certificates authorized it
to engage in air transportation with respect to persons,
property and mail over various routes, including route No.
2 between the co-terminal points New York, New York, and
Newark, New Jersey, and the terminal point Los Angeles,
California, via certain intermediate points, including
Albuquerque, New Mexico, Winslow, Arizona, and Boulder
City, Nevada.

     Flight Personnel: The crew of the flight in question
consisted of Captain Wayne C. Williams, First Officer M.
A. Gillette, and Air Hostess Alice Frances Getz.
     Captain Williams,   aged 41, held an airline transport
pilot certificate.   He had a total of 12,024 hours flying
time, of which approximately 3500 hours had been in DC-3
airplanes.   His night flying time between August 1, 1941,
and the date of the accident was approximately 203 hours.
His last physical examination, required by the Civil Air
Regulations, was taken on December 19, 1941, and showed
him to be in satisfactory physical condition.
     Captain Williams was employed by TWA on September 7,
1931.   The Board examined the facts relating to the dis-
charge of Captain Wayne Williams and his subsequent rein-
statement by TWA after a proceeding held before the then
National Labor Board, and considered their relationship to
the accident.   A request for a rehearing had been granted
but no further proceedings were taken.   Since his rein-
statement and until the time of the accident, Captain Williams' conduct and procedure were considered satisfactory
by the management of TWA.   We therefore conclude that the
dispute between Captain Williams and TWA in 1933 has no
causal relation to the accident.
     Captain Williams originally qualified on all routes
of the Albuquerque-Burbank Division in 1938.[2]   As he was

assigned as pilot on another division, however, this route
qualification expired.   He was requalified on all   routes
between Albuquerque and Burbank,   including the Las Vegas-
Burbank route,   on January 7,   1941, after having complied
with   the requirements of the company and of the Civil Air
Regulations.   He was assigned to the   Albuquerque-Burbank
Division on November 16,   1941.   Since then he had made 39
trips on this division,   seven of which included trips between Burbank and Boulder City,   and two of which included
trips   between   Burbank and Las Vegas.   His   rest   period
prior to departure from Albuquerque on January 16th was 22
hours, 40 minutes.
     First   Officer Gillette,   aged 25,   held a commercial
pilot   certificate   and had a total   flying   time   of   1330
hours,   650   of which had been in DC-3 airplanes.   He was
employed by TWA on August 1, 1940, and was assigned to the
Albuquerque-Burbank Division on February 22,   1941.   Since
then he had made six trips which included landing at,   or
passing over, Las Vegas, and 37 trips which included landing at, or passing over, Boulder City.   He was also qualified   as a reserve first officer on TWA's Boeing S307-B's.
His rest period prior to departure from Albuquerque on the
day of the accident was 15 hours, 24 minutes.
     It   appears from the evidence that both Captain   Wil-
liams   and First Officer Gillette were   physically   qualified,   and   held proper certificates of competency for the
flight involved.

     Airplane and Equipment: Aircraft NC 1946 was a DC-3,
manufactured   by Douglas Aircraft Company Inc.,   of   Santa
Monica,   California.   It was completed February 24, 1941,
and was delivered to TWA March 3,   1941.   The airplane was
powered with two Wright Cyclone G202A engines,   each rated
at   1200 horsepower for take-off,   and was   equipped   with
Hamilton Standard constant speed,   hydromatic, full-feath-
ering   propellers.   This model airplane had been approved
by   the Civil Aeronautics Administration for   air   carrier
operation   over the routes flown by TWA with 24 passengers
and a crew of four.   The evidence indicates that the airplane and its equipment had received the overhauls,   peri-
odic inspections, and checks which are required by company
practice and approved by the Civil Aeronautics Administration,   and that the airplane was in an airworthy condition
on departure from Las Vegas on the day of the accident.
     It is not possible to arrive at a precise   determina-
tion   of the actual gross weight and c.g.   location of the
airplane   at the time it took off from Las Vegas.   As   we
shall explain later,   we can determine only that the gross
weight   of the airplane probably exceeded 25,200   pounds,
which   is   the permissible weight,   by not more   than   500
pounds,   and that the c.g. location probably was within the
prescribed limits.

     History of the Flight: TWA's Flight 3 of January 15,
1942,   enroute   from New York,   New York,   to Los Angeles,

California, departed from Las Vegas, Nevada, at 7:07 p.m.
(PST), January 16, 1942. Approximately 15 minutes later
it collided with an almost verticle rock cliff, near the
top of Potosi Mountain in the Spring Mountain Range. The
point of impact was at an elevation of approximately 7,770
feet above sea level, about 80 feet below the top of the
cliff, and about 730 feet below the crest of the mountain,
which has an elevation of about 8,500 feet above sea
level. The point where the accident occurred is about 33
miles southwest of the Las Vegas airport and 6.7 miles (in
a northwesterly direction) from the center line of the
southwest leg of the Las Vegas radio range.
    The flight had arrived at Albuquerque, New Mexico, at
4:06 p.m. (MST), approximately three hours late as a result of delays at several stations along the route. Most
of these delays had been of 10 or 15 minutes duration and
were occasioned by handling cargo. The longest delay, 1
hour and 56 minutes, occurred at St. Louis, Missouri, due
to weather. In accordance with usual procedure, the crew
which had been in charge was replaced by the crew previously named.
    Flight 3 is regularly scheduled to operate between
Albuquerque, New Mexico, and Burbank, California, without
any intermediate stops. It was planned, however, that
this flight should make intermediate stops at Winslow,
Arizona, and Las Vegas, Nevada,[3] because of reduced fuel
load[4] and reported head winds over the airways. Provision
for these stops was included in the flight plan filed at
Albuquerque.
    The flight was cleared from Albuquerque to Winslow,
the standard TWA clearance form having been completed at
Albuquerque upon receipt of a radio message from TWA's
flight superintendent at Burbank releasing the flight to
Winslow. The airplane departed from Albuquerque at 4:40
p.m. (MST). At 5:38 Captain Williams transmitted the following radio message to Burbank:
    "DEEP LAKE 5:36 8000. WINSLOW 6:04 LAS VEGAS 6:45
    PMP WITH 100 TOTAL. REQUEST RELEASE IN FLIGHT TO LAS
    VEGAS."
The following message was then transmitted to the flight,
over the signature of the flight superintendent at Burbank, the time of the communication being indicated on the
radio log as 4:38 p.m. (PST):
    "PROCEED LAS VEGAS SUBJECT CAPTAIN'S DISCRETION ROUTE
    AC."[5]
    In explanation of this modification of the original
plans, TWA's chief pilot testified that after Captain Williams reached cruising altitude and had an opportunity to
establish ground speed and fuel consumption, he apparently
found that he could continue to Las Vegas, without landing
at Winslow, with a sufficient reserve supply of fuel remaining in the tanks, thus obviating the necessity of an
extra landing and consequent loss of time.
    Flight 3 arrived at Las Vegas at 6:36 (PST) and the
airplane was serviced with fuel. It departed from Las

Vegas at 7:07 p.m., having been cleared to Burbank pursu-
ant to a release transmitted by radio from the Burbank
flight superintendent.

After its departure from Las Vegas the airplane was
observed by several witnesses who stated that it was farther to the northwest than they were accustomed to seeing
the airline planes flying in that vicinity. About 7:22
p.m., 15 minutes after the flight left the ground at Las
Vegas, witnesses observed a fire in the vicinity of Potosi
Mountain, later identified as the fire which occurred in
and about the airplane following impact, and the wreckage
was subsequently found at the location previously described.

Weather Conditions: It is apparent from the evidence
that weather conditions in the area involved were entirely
satisfactory for the flight. United States Weather Bureau
records indicate that the ceiling and visibility were unlimited, with high cloudiness,[6] before, during and after
the flight. These reports were fully substantiated by the
testimony of two Western Air Lines captains who operated
flights in the vicinity of the accident about 1-1/2 hours
after the accident occurred.

Examination of the Wreckage: The examination of the
wreckage did not reveal any evidence of failure of any
part of the airplane or its equipment prior to impact.

It appears probable that the airplane struck the face
of the cliff while approximately level longitudinally and
laterally, and while proceeding straight ahead under
cruising power. The first contact was apparently made by
the left wing with a protruding ledge. The marks or scars
on the cliff, apparently made by the wings, were in approximately level alignment. The position of the wreckage
can be most reasonably explained on the hypothesis that
the impact occurred while the airplane was in a level attitude. Portions of the airplane and of its contents were
found on the top ledge of the cliff, some 80 feet above,
and 400 or 500 feet distant from, the point of impact, a
result which tends to negate the possibility that the airplane was in a diving attitude. On the other hand, the
tops of trees immediately below the point of impact showed
no signs of contact with the airplane, definitely indica-
ting that the airplane was not climbing steeply, although
it could have been in a gradual climb.

Conduct of the Flight: The flight was cleared to fly
contact from Las Vegas to Burbank, having filed a flight
plan which designated 8000 feet above sea level as the
altitude to be used. Because of the emergency conditions
resulting from the war, nearly all of the beacons between
Las Vegas and Silver Lake were inoperative.[7] Section
61.7108 of the Civil Air Regulations provides, and at the
time of the accident provided in part, as follows:

> "The following rules relating to weather conditions
> will govern the dispatching of air carrier aircraft
> in visual-contact operation. No scheduled air car-
> rier aircraft shall be dispatched unless: (c) During
> night operation at least one beacon on the course
> shall be visible from the aircraft at all times, un-
> less otherwise specifically authorized by the Admin-
> istrator."

It is impossible to determine whether, on the night of the
accident, there would not have been at least one beacon on
the course visible at all times from an airplane flying
the route at an altitude of 8000 feet above sea level. It
is not possible to tell, therefore, whether the dispatch-
ing of the flight under contact rules, rather than under
instrument rules which would have required a higher cruising altitude, constituted a violation of the literal reading of the regulation hereinbefore mentioned. The fact
that most of the beacons were extinguished, however, required extra care in the conduct of the flight, both on
the part of the pilot and with respect to others having to
do with the clearance and flight plan. The question of
the use or requisite care by the pilot will be discussed
later. It was incumbent upon the ground personnel particularly to make sure that the pilot was apprised of the
condition of the beacons. The information in this regard
should have been entered on, or attached to, the clearance
which was issued at Las Vegas.[8] Moreover, the proximity
of the proper course to high terrain might well have sug-
gested to the flight superintendent and other responsible
officials of TWA that night contact flights over the portion of the route involved should be operated at a higher
altitude than 8000 feet during the period that those beacons should continue to be inoperative.

We shall now consider the propriety of the course
used by the flight. The center line of the southwest leg
of the Las Vegas radio range has a true bearing of 221 degrees, or a magnetic bearing of 205 degrees, from the
range station. The evidence indicates that a course following this center line, or varying from it by no more
than a few degrees, is the only course considered proper
for flight out of Las Vegas, on the route toward Burbank,
until arrival at a point in the vicinity of the Table
Mountain beacon, at which point it becomes necessary to
assume a magnetic course of approximately 212 degrees in
order to proceed to Silver Lake and on to Daggett.

As a result of restrictions necessitated by military
activities in areas adjacent to the airway, the Civil
Aeronautics Administration, on July 15, 1941, directed a
written notice to TWA, as well as to other carriers, ad-
vising them that it was necessary to confine all operations between Palmdale, California, and Las Vegas, Nevada,
strictly to the airway, and suggesting that pilots be instructed to confine their flight movements, day or night,
contact or instrument, to the actual on-course signal of

the radio ranges serving the airway involved.   A communication directed   to TWA flight personnel by TWA's acting
chief pilot, dated July 17, 1941, incorporated this notice
verbatim and requested pilots to be   guided   accordingly.
Copies   were   posted on flight bulletin boards   at   Kansas
City, Albuquerque, Burbank, and San Francisco.
        The   highest terrain along the correct course between
Las Vegas and Silver Lake appears to be at an elevation of
less than 6000 feet.   The highest point within 15 miles on
either side of the course line is Potosi Mountain,   which,
as previously indicated, rises to an elevation of approximately 8500 feet,   and, while it is located on the airway,
it is off the on-course signal.
        There   was received in evidence at the hearing a   TWA
flight log sheet form covering the route from   Albuquerque
to Burbank,   via Winslow, Arizona,   Boulder City, Nevada,
and Newhall, California.   This flight log sheet is a part
of   the   pilot's   navigation   kit,   and   indicates   proper
courses   for   the various sectors of the route.   It   also
contains a profile chart of the highest terrain along   the
course line and, in addition, the highest terrain within a
strip, 30 miles in width, which extends 15 miles on either
side   of the course line.   The highest terrain   indicated
for   the course line between Boulder City and Silver   Lake
is   approximately 5800 feet,   and the highest point   indicated   within   the 30-mile strip for this section is   9000
feet.   The route between Las Vegas and Silver Lake is also
shown on the log sheet,   and the proper magnetic course is
indicated.   Although no separate profile is provided   for
this route,   it is apparent from what we have said that no
substantially higher terrain exists on this route,   either
on   the   course   line or within 15 miles   on   either   side
thereof,   than is indicated on the log sheet for the course
between Boulder City and Silver Lake.
        With   respect to the altitude to be used for   contact
flight   between   Las Vegas and Burbank,   there appears   to
have been,   at the time of the accident,   no definite rule
prescribed   by TWA.   TWA's chief pilot testified that   it
was the established practice never to operate at less than
1000   feet above the terrain along the   course,   and   that
normally   a pilot   would not fly from   Las Vegas   toward
Silver Lake at less than 8000 feet above sea level, unless
some   weather   condition in the area required flying at   a
lower altitude.
        The   point at which the accident occurred has a bear-
ing of approximately 215 degrees, magnetic, from the Las
Vegas airport, and, as previously indicated, is at an elevation of about 7,770 feet.   In view of the fact that witnesses who observed the plane as it was flying between Las
Vegas and Potosi Mountain testified that its flight path
appeared to be in a straight line northwest of the general
line of flight on which the airline planes usually travel
in   that vicinity,   it appears probable that the   airplane
proceeded   directly   from the airport to the point of   impact.   This conclusion is substantiated by the fact   that

the elapsed time between departure from Las Vegas and the time at which the fire was observed was determined to be a normal amount of time for direct flight between the two points.

The impact actually occurred at an altitude of 7,770 feet above sea-level approximately 15 minutes after take-off from a field at an elevation of 1900 feet. It would appear probably, therefore, that the airplane had been climbing steadily from the time of take-off, and had not quite reached its intended operating altitude at the time of the accident.

Although the airplane, at the time of the accident, was within the limits of the airway, it was 6.7 miles from the center line of the Las Vegas radio range leg. Furthermore, the course being flown, if it were continued, would place the airplane outside the limits of the airway.

It is obvious that, in view of the topography of the area involved, adherence to the course flown, at least at the altitude involved, was not only entirely improper but inevitably led to disaster.

There remains to be determined the reason or reasons for use of the improper course. The flight plan, which covered all portions of the flight from Albuquerque to Burbank, was prepared on the standard TWA form and was filed at Albuquerque. TWA's Operations Manual directs that the flight plan be prepared by the first officer under the supervision of the captain, and that it be approved and signed by the captain. The only name appearing on the flight plan in this instance, however, is that of the first officer which was printed, by hand, in the space provided for the name of the person who prepares the plan. For the first portion of the flight between Las Vegas and Burbank, namely, the sector from Las Vegas to Daggett, the flight plan designated a true course of 234 degrees and a magnetic course of 218 degrees. Since the magnetic bearing of the point of impact from the Las Vegas airport was about 215 degrees, it is apparent that the course flown was substantially the same as the course designated in the flight plan. It would be rather remarkable if the fact that the accident occurred so close to the course designated in the flight plan and at a considerable distance from the proper course were merely a coincidence.

The evidence indicates that in preparing a flight plan the practice is to divide the flight into several portions, each of which may include a number of sectors or legs having separate courses, and to enter on the flight plan for each portion a course which represents the average of the courses of the individual sectors. The result is that a course designated on the flight plan is approximately equivalent to a straight line between the extremities of the portion of the flight for which it is entered.

The average magnetic course between Las Vegas and Daggett is about 210 degrees, rather than 218 degrees which was the course designated in the flight plan. The average magnetic course between Boulder City and Daggett,

on the other hand, is 218 degrees. In view of the fact
that both the captain and the first officer, and particularly the latter (who apparently prepared the flight
plan), had made a substantially larger percentage of
flights via Boulder City than via Las Vegas,[9] it seems
likely that the average course out of Boulder City was inadvertantly designated in the flight plan in place of the
correct average course out of Las Vegas.[10]

The evidence shows that in some instances flights
proceed in approximately a straight line between the extremities of a given portion of the route without following the courses of the individual sectors. Apparently
such practice is customary, under contact conditions, when
the result is to keep the airplane on the right side of
the airway. In any instance in which a direct course is
used, it is apparent that the course flown will be approximately equivalent to the average course indicated on the
flight plan (if the correct average course is entered).

A flight proceeding from Las Vegas to Daggett by direct air line, following a magnetic course of about 210
degrees, would remain on the right side of the airway.
While flight on that course, at the altitude involved,
would place the airplane closer to the higher terrain of
Potosi Mountain than would be the case if the on-course
signal were strictly adhered to, the flight path would
avoid the 8,000-foot level of the higher terrain by a distance of about 3-1/2 miles. Aside from the suggestion
that flights remain within the confines of the on-course
signal in the area, which obviously seems to have been
ignored, there was no company regulation or instruction at
the time of the accident which would prevent the use of
such course. It may well be that the crew of the flight
involved in the accident intended to fly that course, or a
course between it and the on-course signal. If so, it is
quite possible that the average course of 218 degrees,
applicable to the Boulder City-Daggett route, was erroneously utilized, in assuming a heading out of Las Vegas,
in the belief that it was the average or direct line
course between Las Vegas and Daggett.

Except in those cases where one of TWA's flight
superintendents is stationed at the point at which the
flight plan is prepared, the flight plan is not checked by
anyone other than the flight crew. Since there was no
flight superintendent at Albuquerque, the flight plan in
this case was not checked. The fact that the flight plan
involved here contained such a substantial error and the
fact that it was not signed by the captain indicate an ur-
gent need for a closer watch over such irregularities.

Whatever may have been the fact with respect to the
use of the flight plan course, it seems obvious that Captain Williams and First Officer Gillette were paying no
more than slight attention to the position of the airplane
by visual reference to objects on the ground.

Although, as previously mentioned, certain beacons on
the route were inoperative due to the emergency conditions

resulting from the war, one of the five beacons between Las Vegas and Silver Lake was lighted on the night of the accident. Beacon 24, also referred to as the Arden Beacon, which is located along the route about 20 miles from the Las Vegas airport, was operating. This beacon is about 2-1/2 miles to the right of the center line of the Las Vegas radio range leg. Flights southwest bound out of Las Vegas should pass to the left of the beacon, but the flight involved in the accident apparently flew past on the right. In this connection it may be noted that Captain Williams' last preceding flight from Las Vegas to Burbank was made on the night of December 21, 1941, at which time Beacon 24, as well as the other beacons in the area, were unlighted. It may be that he erroneously assumed that he was approximately on course as he flew to the right of it. In addition to this lighted beacon, however, the lights of the town of Arden and of automobiles on U. S. Highway No. 91, and farther on, the lights of the town of Goodsprings, afforded reliable reference points. Moreover, under contact conditions such as existed on the night of the accident, if the cockpit lights are kept dimmed, it is possible to see the outline of the mountains, especially when the peaks are snow-covered as they were on January 16.

Furthermore, it appears from the radio range monitor reports that the available radio range facilities were operating properly at the time of the accident. Had the captain and first officer been listening to the Las Vegas radio range, a moderate "A" signal would have been heard, which would have definitely indicated that the airplane was off course. Despite the suggestion hereinbefore mentioned that flights remain within the limits of the on-course signal in the area involved, it seems obvious that the pilots were not using the radio range for navigational purposes.

III. Conclusion

Findings: We find, upon all of the evidence available to the Board at this time, that the facts relating to the accident involving aircraft NC 1946, which occurred near Las Vegas, Nevada, on January 16, 1942, are as follows:

1. The accident, which occurred at approximately 7:20 p.m. (PST) to Flight 3 of Transcontinental & Western Air, Inc., resulted in fatal injuries to the 19 passengers and crew of 3 and in destruction of the airplane.

2. At the time of the accident Transcontinental & Western Air, Inc. held a currently effective certificate of public convenience and necessity and an air carrier operating certificate authorizing it to conduct the flight.

3. Captain Williams and First Officer Gillette were physically qualified and held proper certificates of com-

petency to perform their duties on the flight in question.
    4. Aircraft NC 1946 was currently certificated as
airworthy at the time of the accident.
    5. The flight plan for Flight 3, filed at Albuquer-
que, New Mexico, designated a magnetic course of 218 degrees for the portion of the route between Las Vegas,
Nevada, and Daggett, California. The average of the
courses of the sectors comprising the route between Las
Vegas and Daggett is about 210 degrees. 8000 feet above
sea level was the altitude designated in the flight plan.
    6. Flight 3 departed from Las Vegas, Nevada, at 7:07
p.m. having been cleared to fly in accordance with contact
flight rules to Burbank, California.
    7. About 15 minutes after departure from Las Vegas,
Nevada, the airplane collided with Potosi Mountain, in the
Spring Mountain Range of Nevada, at an elevation of 7,770
feet above sea level, while approximately level longitudinally and laterally and while proceeding straight ahead
approximately at cruising speed. The point of impact has
a magnetic bearing of approximately 215 degrees from the
Las Vegas airport.
    8. The airplane was flown between Las Vegas, Nevada,
and the point of impact on a course which was improper for
the route involved.
    9. Weather conditions in the area at the time were
entirely satisfactory for the flight.
    10. The available radio range facilities were opera-
ting normally at the time of the accident.
    11. Due to emergency conditions resulting from the
war, only one beacon between Las Vegas, Nevada, and Silver
Lake, California, was operating.
    12. There was no evidence of structural, control sys-
tem, or power plant failure prior to the accident, and the
engines and propellers were functioning normally at the
time the aircraft struck the mountain.

    Probable Cause: Upon the basis of the foregoing
findings and of the entire record available at this time,
we find that the probable cause of the accident to aircraft NC 1946 on January 16, 1942, was the failure of the
captain after departure from Las Vegas to follow the proper course by making use of the navigational facilities
available to him.

    Contributing Factors:
    1. The use of an erroneous compass course.
    2. Blackout of most of the beacons in the neighbor-
hood of the accident made necessary by the war emergency.
    3. Failure of the pilot to comply with TWA's direc-
tive of July 17, 1941, issued in accordance with a suggestion from the Administrator of Civil Aeronautics request-
ing pilots to confine their flight movements to the actual
on-course signals.

    Comment and Recommendations: The investigation of

this accident has indicated the need for more precise and specific operational procedures and regulatory standards with respect to contact night flight. Accordingly, the Board has submitted the following recommendation to the Administrator:

> "It is therefore recommended that the Administrator of Civil Aeronautics establish, for inclusion in the operations manual of air carriers, such contact flight procedures at each airport as will insure that the climb to, and descent from, cruising altitude be conducted at a safe distance from all obstructions."

As further remedial measures in this regard, the Board is now considering proposed regulations which would require night contact flights to (1) remain within the confines of the proper twilight zone of the on-course signal, and (2) fly at an altitude not less than 1000 feet above the highest obstacle located within a horizontal distance of 10 miles from the center of the course intended to be flown.

The preparation of flight plans obviously should be regarded as more than mere routine. The possibility of irregularities such as those which occurred in connection with the preparation of the flight plan involved in this instance should be eliminated. All airlines which do not now have procedures which call for an adequate check of flight plans should establish them. The company's operation manual required the captain to approve and sign the flight plan; nevertheless, the Board is considering the promulgation of a regulation which would make it a violation not to do so.

Every airline should also maintain a closer control on the determination of the gross weight and c.g. location of an airplane. If an average weight is used, either for all the passengers or for any group of passengers, it ought to be taken seriously enough to prevent the casual acceptance, on indirect information, of an intrinsically improbable figure. If the weight of the passengers is computed on an actual weight basis, it is obviously necessary that reasonable diligence be exercised by the station personnel to ascertain from the passengers their correct weights.

Approved:

L. Welch Pogue
Harllee Branch
Oswald Ryan
Edward Warner

Baker, Member, did not take part in the decision.

Footnotes:

[1] This investigator was contacted, early on the morning following the accident, at Amarillo, Texas, where he was enroute from Washington, D. C., to Los Angeles, California. He proceeded to Las Vegas by the most expeditious transportation available and reached the scene of the accident with the second party to arrive, consisting of Civil Aeronautics Administration inspectors, postal inspectors, TWA officials, civil officers and a military detachment.

[2] Burbank, California, is TWA's terminal airport serving Los Angeles.

[3] When operating over this route, daylight landings are made at Boulder City rather than Las Vegas, but night landings are made at Las Vegas because there are no lights at the Boulder City Airport.

[4] Due to the heavy passenger and cargo load, the airplane was fueled to depart from Albuquerque with only 350 gallons of gasoline. It appears that the weight of the airplane, on departure from Albuquerque and also on departure from Las Vegas, was not within the permissable gross weight according to the regular method of computation. It is not possible to determine precisely the amount of the excess, but in all probability it was less than 500 pounds. The excess was due principally to the method which was used to assign passenger weights in computing the load at Albuquerque. The regular method of computation calls for the use of an average weight of 170 pounds per passenger, exclusive of baggage. TWA's passenger agent at Albuquerque testified that since computation on this basis resulted in a weight which was greater than the permissable weight, he requested the officer in charge of the 12 Army men getting on at Albuquerque to state the weights of these men. An average weight of 150 pounds was assigned to each of the 12 men. Finding that the total weight was still too heavy, the agent contacted the three women passengers and obtained and used their actual weights. Since the computation then indicated that the gross weight of the airplane precisely equaled the provisional weight permissible for take-off, the remaining passengers were figured at 170 pounds each without inquiry as to their actual weights. Army records show that the Army personnel actually weighed substantially more than the amount assigned for them. The overweight would not seem to have had any bearing on the accident. The method used for computing the load, and, therefore, of ascertaining the location of the c.g., however, is an example of loose practice, and of a ready acceptance (where such acceptance served to avoid interference with the handling of traffic) of an intrinsically improbable statement (that a considerable group of adult

men would have an average weight as low as 150 lbs. each).

[5]"AC" is TWA's designation of the Winslow-Kingman-Las Vegas route.

[6]High cloudiness is not inconsistent with the existence of unlimited ceiling and visibility. Ceiling is considered unlimited when clouds cover less than one-half of the sky or when the base of the clouds is more than 9,750 feet above the point of observation. Visibility is the mean greatest distance toward the horizon that prominent objects can be seen and identified by the normal eye. Visibility is considered unlimited when its extent is 10 miles or more.

[7]Beacon Nos. 19, 21, 23/A and 23B, or the Francis Spring, Kingston Pass, Table Mountain, and Wilson Pass beacons, were unlighted.

[8]Section 61.71042 of the Civil Air Regulations provides in part as follows: "(c) The dispatcher or duly authorized station personnel shall attach or enter all current reports or information pertaining to weather and irregularities of navigational aids and facilities...affecting the flight."

[9]Captain Williams had made 7 trips between Burbank and Boulder City and 2 trips between Burbank and Las Vegas. First Officer Gillette had made 37 trips via Boulder City and 6 trips via Las Vegas.

[10]During the investigation other flight plans prepared by TWA pilots for flights over the route were examined. One was discovered in which the course designated for the Las Vegas-Daggett portion was 218 degrees, i.e., the same as the course designated in the instant case. TWA's chief pilot testified that this was obviously a mistake.

Bibliography

Included in this section are books and magazine articles that can be considered *principal sources* on the subject of Carole Lombard. Brief summaries of her life and career (such as those found in most film reference books) are not included; nor are newspaper articles as these would be a) nearly impossible to list in their entirety, and b) self-explanatory in nature. For instance, relevant dates can be consulted in any newspaper for information on, say, the death of Russ Columbo on September 2, 1934, the marriage of Lombard and Gable on March 29, 1939, or the death of Carole Lombard on January 16, 1942. Therefore, newspaper sources need not be cited here. Their coverage is fairly standard on any subject, limited in interpretation, and predictable regarding dates. For a concise representation of newspaper dates, consult *The New York Times Index*, available at larger libraries. Sources listed here are also confined to those issued within the United States; a bibliography that includes foreign works would be partial at best, with these sources difficult to obtain. The listing of American magazines is as complete as possible, given the scarcity of some titles issued in the 1920s and 1930s.

Film portrayals of Lombard *are* listed here. These include documentaries about Lombard and/or Gable, and dramatic representations of old Hollywood on both the large and small screens. In 1987, Darrah Meeley Productions created a Carole Lombard retrospective for the Women In Film Festival, held at the Universal City Cinemas. This film included reminiscences of Lombard by Robert Stack, Lucille Ball, and others, plus the Lombard collection of Susan Marie Rice of Glendale, California. It was possible, as of early 1988, that the film would be re-edited for sale to television; as this book goes to press, no final decision regarding its future has been reached.

BOOKS

001 Behlmer, Rudy, ed. *Memo from David O. Selznick*. New York: The Viking Press, 1972.

Significant in the context of the *cold war* between Clark Gable and David Selznick following production of *Gone With the Wind*. Lombard considered herself an unwilling victim caught in the middle, and this is reflected in a long letter to her from Selznick that read in part: "...there is something I would like to discuss with you very frankly. Are you sure, Carole, that we should make another picture together? I know from countless sources how highly you think of me, both as a person and a producer, and this is a source of great satisfaction to me...Certainly I have always held you up as the shining example of what a joy it can be to work with a star when that star appreciates a producer's problems and cooperates in their solution. But I must face the fact that you are married to Clark, and that Clark obviously feels quite differently about me...I certainly recognize the awkward position you are in, and cannot expect to come out on the right side when your loyalties are divided." Lombard never did complete her obligation to Selznick; ironically, while on a bombing mission over Germany long after Carole's death, Gable resolved to apologize to Selznick and did so. Editor Rudy Behlmer quotes Gable as thinking to himself about Selznick, "What did that guy ever do to me except force me to be in the most important film I ever made? If I get out of here alive, I'm going to apologize."

002   *Carole Lombard's Life Story*. 1942.

A thirty-four page magazine tribute published shortly after the star's death; profusely illustrated, including extremely rare photos. Although no author credit is given, from clues provided in the text it is likely the author was Louella Parsons or another columnist of similar stature.

003   Carr, Larry. *More Fabulous Faces*. Garden City: Doubleday and Co., 1979.

Lombard is one of five actresses chronicled in this coffee-table book. The 45 page chapter features biographical text and 160 photos of various sizes.

004   Chierichetti, David. *Hollywood Director: the Career Mitchell Leisen*. New York: Curtis Books, 1973.

This very rare book amounts to one of the finest sources ever written about Lombard as it contains page after page of rare quotes from her close friend Mitch Leisen as well as co-star Fred MacMurray and others. Contains descriptions of the filming of *The Eagle and the Hawk, Hands Across the Table*, and *Swing High, Swing Low*. Of MacMurray and Lombard in *Hands Across the Table*, Leisen said, "Fred had a natural flair for comedy, but he was terribly shy in those days and he was afraid to try any-

thing.   We really had to draw it out of him, and Carole
was a great help there.   She worked as hard as I did   to
get that performance out of him.   She had none of what you
might call the 'star temperament.'   She felt that all   the
others had to be good or it wouldn't matter how good   she
was."   And Leisen's moving comments about Lombard's death
bear reprinting: "I was still in bed one morning when my
wife came in with the news that Carole's plane had
crashed...I went into a state of shock when I   heard   the
news...and I went down to the studio in a daze.   The only
person I talked to all day was Claudette Colbert.   She was
devastated too.   Finally she led me behind a flat on some
soundstage and said,   'Nobody's looking. You can let go.'
I cried.   I had to leave the studio.   I spent the whole
day at the beach, walking up and down, looking at the
waves.   I could not make myself believe that Carole wasn't
there anymore.   I haven't gotten over it yet, and I never
will."

005   Crosby,   Bing as told to Pete Martin. *Call Me Lucky*.
      New York: Simon and Schuster, 1953.

006   Essoe, Gabe.   *The Films of Clark Gable*.   Secaucus:
      The Citadel Press, 1969.

      Loaded with information, as are most *Films of* vol-
umes,   although Essoe's biographical section about Gable
contains some sloppy, inaccurate Lombard references.   The
14 Lombard photos included are excellent.

007   Finch,   Christopher and Linda Rosenkrantz.   *Gone
      Hollywood: the Movie Colony in the Golden Age*.
      Garden City: Doubleday and Co., 1979.

      More than 40 short references to Carole Lombard   are
made in this 396 page volume of facts, legends,   and
trivia.   Includes 3 Lombard photographs.

008   Francisco,   Charles.   *Gentleman: the William Powell
      Story*. New York: St. Martin's Press, 1985.

      This small biography offers a by-the-numbers   recon-
struction of Powell's association with Lombard.   It is accurate in its facts but never delves beneath the surface
of its characters.   Includes 5 photos of Lombard and
Powell.

009   Gable,   Kathleen.   *Clark Gable: a Personal Portrait*.
      Englewood Cliffs: Prentice-Hall, Inc., 1961.

      In October,   1942, nine months after Lombard's death,
Gable met Kathleen Williams,   then a model and bit player.
13 years later they married, and 6 years after that, Kay
Gable rushed this Gable post mortem into print.   There is
an eerie quality to this volume, as if the author   credit

should read, "with Kathleen Gable as Carole Lombard." The tone is somewhat snobbish and unsentimental as Kay shares her memories of Clark, with all roads leading back to herself. Lombard is mentioned only briefly but her presence is felt in photos and descriptions of the Encino ranch. Kay Gable emerges through this volume as a roadshow version of Lombard, down to her self-professed no-nonsense spunk and the way she referred to Clark as "Pa."

010   Garceau, Jean with Inez Cocke. *Dear Mr. G.* Boston: Little, Brown and Co., 1961.

Fully one-half of Garceau's memoir details her association with Lombard from 1938 to 1942 as secretary and business manager, a position she soon also held for Gable. The account is saccharine in places but does present a unique look at the Lombard-Gable home life, particularly as regards the Encino ranch.

011   Garceau, Jean with Inez Cocke. *Gable: a Pictorial Biography*. New York: Grosset and Dunlop, 1977.

A reprint of 1961's *Dear Mr. G.*, this time including photos that *should* have graced the earlier edition. In addition to the dozens of photos of Gable, there are 24 including Lombard. Many came from the Gable, Lombard, and Garceau personal collections.

012   Gargan, William. *Why Me? An Autobiography*. Garden City: Doubleday and Co., 1969.

013   Harris, Warren G. *Gable and Lombard*. New York: Simon and Schuster, 1974.

A romantic, sentimental, and superficial examination of the famous romance that became a commercial success in spite of itself. Includes 14 pages of photographs. The *Library Journal* said this book "has no acceptable analysis of the gifted Lombard's movie career or of what made Gable the male sex symbol of his time and it tells us nothing about the special nature of Hollywood stardom in the first decade of the talkies. The psychological insights are banal, and the book dumps on Marilyn Monroe unnecessarily. But movie-star biographies, although they're usually terrible, are widely read in libraries and *Gable and Lombard,* affectionately written and full of Hollywood gossip, is a lot better than most. Lombard, especially, is an irresistible subject."

014   Haver, Ronald. *David O. Selznick's Hollywood*. New York: Alfred A. Knopf, 1980.

Huge coffee-table volume detailing the career of Selznick. Includes descriptions of the productions of *Nothing Sacred* and *Made for Each Other*. Lombard's

closeness to Selznick International and the production of
Gone With the Wind lead to several other references.
Includes 5 color photos.

015 Hayne, Donald, ed. *The Autobiography of Cecil B.
     DeMille.* Englewood Cliffs: Prentice Hall, 1959.

016 Head, Edith and Jane Kesner Ardmore. *The Dress
     Doctor.* Boston: Little, Brown and Co., 1959.

     Head states, "More than once I was about to give no-
tice [at the Paramount Studios]...The patient who really
influenced me to stay was Carole Lombard...here was something different: the first fashion-conscious star I'd
met, one who could influence the taste of the American
woman...The girls in the workroom worshipped her, the fit-
ters begged to work with her. That's a true
barometer...Her fittings were gay, hilarious, you could
hear them for six blocks off. She had great clothes sense
and a true clotheshorse figure, but she didn't take
clothes or herself seriously. Nothing was sacred, not
even the third act of *Camille*; nothing was a crisis...I'd
seen Travis Banton, in the years he'd worked with Carole,
transform her from a salesgirl to a duchess, all in modern
dress. Now, in his absence, I was doing it, creating
little sheath suits that enhanced her lean, clean grey-
hound look. I've loved suits ever since, and the Lombard
look. I began to realize what you could do with smart
clothes. Like any novice I began to dream of Miracles."
Head came in contact with nearly all the greats during her
remarkable career. The two pages she devotes to Carole
are quite evocative.

017 Heimann, Jim. *Out with the Stars: Hollywood Night-
     life in the Golden Era.* New York: Abbeyville Press,
     1985.

     Featuring Lombard and Gable on its cover, this eclec-
tic volume describes all of Hollywood's best nightspots.
Several references are made to Lombard, whose favorite
haunts included the Brown Derby and Trocadero, and she is
pictured twice.

018 Holzer, Hans. *Star Ghosts.* New York: Leisure Books,
     1979.

     Not everyone believes in ghosts. Not everyone be-
lieves in Hans Holzer. Still, if there is any validity to
the concept of ghosts and hauntings, Carole Lombard is a
prime candidate because of her sudden, unexpected and vio-
lent death. Holzer, based on alleged sightings of a ghost
in Carole's Hollywood Boulevard home, held a seance there
with a medium he refers to as "Julie Parrish." A spirit
with blonde hair, wearing a red dress allegedly appeared
to Ms. Parrish and kept laughing at the people holding the

seance, repeatedly wondering why they had brought her to that particular house. In recent years, after the publication of this book, it has been discovered that the seance was held at the wrong house on Hollywood Boulevard; something of which Holzer may still be unaware, yet a reasonable mistake since two homes there have the same unusual facade. With this in mind, the plot thickens, and the spirit in the red dress, the one laughing at Holzer and his medium, wondering why they had summoned her to that house, gains a certain amount of credibility. An entire chapter is devoted to Lombard's ghost and the seance held on Hollywood Boulevard.

019 Hotchner, A. E. *Choice People: the Greats, Near-Greats and Ingrates I Have Known.* New York: William Morrow and Co., 1984.

Hemingway's biographer tackles, among others, Clark Gable. The story is a poignant one: Gable in World War II, talking emotionally about Lombard, including making love in the duck blinds, her death, and the locket he wore around his neck which contained a fragment of one of her pieces of ruby and diamond jewelry.

020 Jordan, Rene. *Clark Gable.* New York: Pyramid Publications, 1973.

A thoroughly routine look at Gable's life, with utterly predicatable references to Lombard.

021 Kanin, Garson. *Hollywood.* New York: The Viking Press, 1974.

In several vivid passages, the brilliant Mr. Kanin perfectly captures the experience of working, sharing conversations, friendships, and love with Carole Lombard. A brief period, from 1940 to 1942, is covered.

022 Maltin, Leonard. *Carole Lombard.* New York: Pyramid Publications, 1976.

Maltin's work is typically thoughtful, accurate in every detail and includes many appropriate quotes from friends and co-workers. Profusely illustrated, with filmography.

023 Milland, Ray. *Wide-eyed in Babylon.* New York: William Morrow and Co., 1974.

Milland's descriptions stem from working with Carole on two films in 1934. He calls her "...a smashing girl, a true original and a hell of an actress. When she was annoyed, her language was that of a stevedore. She loved practical jokes and could tell a bawdy story with the best of them. In any company, her taste was impeccable."

Milland credits Lombard as the peacemaker following George
Raft's famous KO of producer Benjamin Glazer; Milland also
recounts a wrap party thrown in her dressing room on
Christmas Eve, 1933, and mentions various incidents that
took place during filming of *We're Not Dressing*.

024   Morella, Joe and Edward Z. Epstein. *Gable and
      Lombard and Powell and Harlow*.   New York: Dell Pub-
      lishing Co., 1976.

A paperback original designed to tie in with the film
Gable and Lombard, this book concerning the four stars and
their interchangeable relationships is well-researched and
written in a gossipy, highly engrossing style.   Hollywood's sordid underbelly is exposed here, although all
four characters come out well. The theme can be summed up
in this excerpt from Chapter 1:   "Gable. Lombard.
Powell.   Harlow. The all-consuming love affairs of these
vital, pampered, passionate human beings had captured and
held the imaginations of moviegoers throughout the world.
They were sex symbols of their time, lovers and mates in
the fabulous world of genuine make-believe that was Hollywood in the 1930s...They were unique, ambitious indivi-
duals who thrust their way to movie stardom. All Midwest-
erners, they were as American as apple pie--but definitely
not the folks next door." The book takes off from here,
stimulating the prurient interest lurking in us all.   Includes many excellent, previously unpublished photos.

025   Niven, David. *Bring on the Empty Horses*. New York:
      G. P. Putnam's Sons, 1975.

David Niven, who never let the truth get in the way
of a good story, looks wistfully at Clark Gable in a chapter entitled "The King," and in so doing shares several
memories of Lombard as well.   Gable told Niven, "Carole
thinks you're a pain in the ass," yet Niven's impression
of her is a positive one.   He is one of few to take note
of her pre-war condemnations of Hitler, and says he was
invited to the Encino ranch for a farewell dinner before
he went to fight in the war in September, 1939.

026   Ott, Frederick W. *The Films of Carole Lombard*.
      Secaucus: The Citadel Press, 1972.

One of the better entries of the *Films of* series,
this volume presents a nearly complete filmography
including casts, credits, running times, photos, plot
synopses, and excerpted reviews. The biography section is
surprisingly in-depth, considering the space alloted.

027   Parish, James Robert. *Paramount Pretties*. Secaucus:
      Castle Books, 1972.

This large volume profiles 16 actresses, Lombard

among them, in separate chapters. The biography concen-
trates on her career, and filmography and still sections
are enclosed. Parish and staff continue to be premiere
film historians; their volumes are uniformly excellent.

028 Parsons, Louella. *Tell It to Louella*. New York:
     G. P. Putnam's Sons, 1961.

Louella, who like David Niven never let the truth
damage an otherwise entertaining reminiscence, recounts
her experiences with Gable and Lombard. She claims to
have witnessed most of the major events in their lives,
which may or may not be apocryphal. Approximately five
pages deal with Carole; these are standard remembrances.

029 Peary, Danny. *Close-ups: the Movie Star Book*. New
     York: Workman Publishing Co., 1979.

Under the heading *The Comics,* Lombard is paid tribute
by director Sidney Salkow in an affectionate 4 page piece
entitled "Carole Lombard: Blithe Spirit." In it, he gives
a unique viewpoint on experiences with Carole while making
Supernatural. Otherwise, the piece slips back into the
same tired old rehash of the Lombard legend.

030 Quinn, Anthony. *The Original Sin*. Boston: Little,
     Brown and Co., 1972.

Quinn's memories of Lombard concern his beginnings at
Paramount working on *Swing High, Swing Low* and reflect his
attraction to Lombard, her consideration of this "rookie,"
and her advice to him concerning career strategy.

031 Ritchie, Donald. *George Stevens: an American Roman-
     tic*. New York: Museum of Modern Art, 1970.

032 St. Johns, Adela Rogers. *Love, Laughter, and Tears:
     My Hollywood Story*. New York: Doubleday and Co.,
     1978.

Recollections of Lombard's oft-time interviewer St.
Johns, who worked as a stringer for the fan magazines of
the late 1930s and 40s.

033 Samuels, Charles. *The King: a Biography of Clark
     Gable*. New York: Coward-McCann, Inc., 1961.

Samuels calls Carole a "human torpedo" in this uneven
account of Gable's exploits written to cash in on the
star's death. The Lombard presented here is accurate, although factual errors crop up often, perhaps testimony to
the rush to publication. An Indianapolis *News* reporter is
quoted as saying of Lombard, "She looks New Yorkish, talks
Bostonish, and acts very Londonish. In manner, she is
brisk and slangy--an attitute which belies her fragile

type of beauty." No photographs are included in the volume.

034 Sennett, Mack and Cameron Ship. *The King of Comedy*.
     Garden City: Doubleday and Co., 1954.

035 Stack, Robert with Mark Evans. *Straight Shooting*.
     New York: Macmillan Publishing Co., 1980.

     Stack's memories of Lombard, which date from his
early adolescence, are positive and impressive. In one
passage he relates the nerve-racking experience of shooting a still session with Carole for *To Be or Not to Be,*
and here uncovers her warmth and caring: "...a wind
machine and a small rapid-sequence Rolleiflex appeared.
Suddenly, with the wind machine roaring and her blond mane
flowing behind her, she started our still session by
throwing her arms around my neck and almost strangling me.
'Loosen up, professor,' she said, shaking me for good
measure.   'We're supposed to be having fun.' We did."
One of the better Hollywood autobiographies, it includes
two photos of Lombard taken in 1933 plus a series of
Lombard-Stack stills from the aforementioned sitting.

036 Swindell, Larry. *Screwball: the Life of Carole
     Lombard*. New York: William Morrow and Co., 1975.

     Screwball is meticulously researched but met with
limited success because of the author's eccentric style of
writing.   Although this must be considered the ultimate
biography of Lombard, it still fails to capture the
driving force of her personality. The book received mixed
reviews; *Library Journal* said, "Lombard generously fed a
legend that continues to obstruct impartial accounts of
her. Nevertheless, Swindell provides many details in this
carefully balanced portrait.   One only regrets that the
biography lacks the sassy style and charm characteristic
of its exuberant subject." The New York *Times Book Review*
said,   "The book is filled with anecdotes that delineate
Lombard's reputation as Hollywood's good-time girl.   They
revolve around her celebrated four-letter-word vocabulary,
her parties...and, of course, Gable...Swindell is fairly
restrained with more sensational gossip...*Screwball* strad-
dles an uneasy line between fan-magazine and authentic
biography and doesn't really make it as either.   The book
is also hampered by an awkward style that is occasionally
obtrusive.   Still, Swindell doesn't betray the Lombard
credo; he gives the reader a pretty good time." Includes
a filmography and 28 pages of photos.

037 Thomas, Bob. *Selznick*. Garden City: Doubleday and
     Co., 1970.

038 Thompson, Charles. *Bing: an Authorized Biography*.
     New York: David McKay Co., 1975.

References to Lombard concern the filming of *We're Not Dressing*. Mention is also made of the Lombard-Russ Columbo relationship.

039 Tornabene, Lyn. *Long Live the King*. New York: G. P. Putnam's Sons, 1976.

Easily the best of the many Gable biographies. Tornabene's work delves deeply into the lives of both Gable and Lombard. The result is an extremely intimate look at Lombard, including both positive and negative aspects of her character. For example, she quotes Gable's pal Johnny Mahin as saying, "There was so much for to her than the swearing; that's what made me mad. She could be a gracious, charming woman. But I hate to be around girls who say shit and fuck. I hate it. I was always uncomfortable. I'd get up and leave. Carole always embarrassed me. Everything was fuck and shit, fuck and shit." Likewise, Tornabene's comments attributed to Margaret Tallichet Wyler, also on the subject of Lombard's off-color language are equally enlightening: "I used to puzzle about it because I found it so *unusual*. I was young and not terribly perceptive, but even then I understood that it had to have begun as a sort of defense mechanism...I felt then, and I feel now, that that was the defense she built for herself so as not to be as vulnerable as she probably was." Tornabene emerges as a writer with a talent for producing spellbinding interviews; rare quotes from tennis ace Alice Marble stand as another highlight, as do the cross-section of opinions from the couple's circle of friends. Includes 5 pages of Lombard-Gable photographs. All in all, one of the best word portraits of Carole Lombard ever painted.

040 Truffaut, Francois. *Hitchcock*. New York: Simon and Schuster, 1967.

The reference to Lombard here is not long but it is notable. In Q and A fashion Truffaut asks Hitchcock about *Mr. and Mrs. Smith*, at which point the director launches off on a tangent about his "actors are cattle" remark, including Lombard's practical joke on that theme.

041 Turner, Lana. *Lana: the Lady, the Legend, the Truth*. New York: E. P. Dutton, 1982.

Significant mainly because of Turner's role in causing unrest in the marriage of Gable and Lombard, *Lana* presents the view of "the other woman." She boldly states that the legendary affair she allegedly shared with Gable never took place, and expresses regret at the rumor that she inadvertantly caused Lombard's death.

042 Wayne, Jane Ellen. *Gable's Women*. New York: Prentice-Hall, 1987.

Gable's Women is at times haunting in its accuracy, at times suspicious in its dialogues between long-dead stars, and once in a while incompetently written. On the whole it offers an accurate, intimate look at Lombard and her relationship with Gable.

043 Weinberg, Herman G.   *The Lubitsch Touch*. New York: E. P. Dutton, 1968.

Examines the Lubitsch-Lombard association, including the making of *To Be or Not to Be*.

044 Wilkerson, Tichi and Marcia Borie.   *The Hollywood Reporter*. New York: Arlington House, 1984.

This compilation of thirty years of the best of *THR* includes dozens of newsy items on Lombard as well as a reprint of her article regarding her publicity work for Selznick. (See Chapter 4).

045 Yablonsky, Lewis.   *George Raft*. New York: McGraw-Hill Book Co., 1974.

Warm reminiscences of Lombard by Raft and his assis-tant Mack Grey.   Details the period of time between the filming of *Bolero* and *Rumba*. (See Chapter 4).

MAGAZINE ARTICLES

046 Albert, Katherine.   "Glamour Girl Plus."   *Picture Play*, Dec. 1938, pp. 24-25, 68.

An excellent sampler of the Lombard personality that details such trivia as her favorite expressions: "She listens as hard as she talks, not wanting to miss a word and emphasizing everything you say with a brisk, 'Yah, yah, I get you' or 'That's right.'...'It's O.K. by me,' is, in essence, one of her favorite expressions."

047 Baral, Robert. "Home Town Stories of the Stars." *New Movie*, Sept. 1931, pp. 7071, 121.

In-depth profile from Fort Wayne, Indiana native Baral on the childhood of Lombard and her family back-ground.

048 Baral, Robert. "Blonde Beauty Grows Up." *Photoplay*, May 1939, pp. 34-35, 91.

Written by childhood acquaintance Baral of Fort Wayne, this extremely brief article, lavishly illustrated, offers a glimpse of Lombard's early years and home town. It is basically a rewrite of the 1931 article.

049   Baskette, Kirtley. "'Scoop' Lombard's One Wild Week."
       Movie Mirror, Nov. 1938, pp. 46-48, 71-73.

       Chronicles Lombard's screwball week as Selznick's
publicity chief in entertaining detail. A long piece,
possibly the best of those written on this subject.
Baskette would soon fall out of Carole's good graces with
his scandalous *Photoplay* article of two months later.

050   Baskette, Kirtley. "Hollywood's Unmarried Husbands
       and Wives." *Photoplay*, Jan. 1939, pp. 22-23, 74.

       Infamous article that shadow-boxed with the issue of
stars "shacking up" without actually landing any blows.
Still, it caused quite a furor in Hollywood with its detailing of the relationships of, among others, Lombard and
Gable.

051   Belfrage, Cedric. "A Teddy-Made Actress." *Motion
       Picture*, May 1929, pp. 59, 102-103.

       Written as hype for C. B. DeMille's film *Dynamite*,
this article includes upbeat quotes by Lombard about
DeMille, who would soon fire her from the production.

052   Benjamin, Louis Paine. "Gawkiness to Glamour."
       Ladies Home Journal, May 1938, pp. 32, 114.

       A brief sketch of Lombard including a few beauty
tips.

053   Bentley, Janet. "She Gets Away with Murder." *Photo-
       play*, March 1938, pp. 27, 88-89.

       An examination of Lombard's business sense and her
stature in the film community, written while she was
making *Fools for Scandal*. "Today, then," wrote Bentley,
Carole is her own free agent; virtually, an artistic
dictator who doesn't have to make a picture for anybody
unless all matters are arranged to suit her. So it's no
wonder, really, that people are gasping." She quotes
Lombard as saying, "You know, the reason that more people
don't get more things they feel they deserve is because
they're afraid to ask for them."

054   "Best Dressed Star." *Movie Classic*, May 1935, p. 28.

       No information available.

055   Biery, Ruth. "Hollywood's Newest Romance." *Photo-
       play*, June 1931, pp. 49, 106.

       Written a few months before their wedding, this en-
lightening and ironic piece reflects Lombard's doubts
about marrying William Powell--something she went ahead

and did, despite her better judgement. And lived to re-gret.

056 Biery, Ruth. "Why Carole Changed Her Mind." *Photo-play,* Sept. 1931, pp. 55, 104-105.

Details the history of the Powell-Lombard relation-ship at a point just after their wedding. Powell's obses-sion with his bride is best summed up with this quote: "I--something is happening to me. It is as though I were breaking down inside. I see life differently. I am dif-ferent. I love Carole. I can think only of Carole."

057 Biery, Ruth. "Carole Lombard Admits the Truth About Her Divorce." *Screen Play,* Dec. 1933, pp. 39, 56.

Another installment in Biery's ongoing inside look at the Lombard-Powell relationship, including wistful quotes by Lombard such as, "We were like two parallel lines. Lines that run along side by side but never come really together. In marriage there can be no parallels. One must blend completely into the other. Neither of us could do that. And if one tried to bend the other it meant that one would break. We would have become deadly enemies through that effort. We did not want that."

058 Binyon, Claude. "Subject: Lombard." *Photoplay,* Jan. 1940, pp. 17, 77.

This short but entertaining piece conveys the humor of Lombard's character, as viewed by the screenwriter of *True Confession.*

059 Biographical note; filmography. *Movies and People,* 1940, p. 23.

No information available.

060 "Boy Gets Girl." *Time,* 10 April 1939, pp. 52-53.

A brief, not-entirely-accurate recap of the Lombard-Gable romanced followed by an announcement of their wed-ding. Photo included.

061 Bruce, Carter. "Sophisticated at Sixteen." *Modern Screen,* July 1931, pp. 76, 108-109.

Lombard looks back candidly at her childhood and ado-lescence, including her unusual relationship with her mother and brothers, and her attraction to older men.

062 Busch, Noel F. "A Loud Cheer for the Screwball Girl." *Life,* 17 Oct. 1938, pp. 48-51, 62-64.

The most complete article, *Life*'s cover story for

that issue, ever written on Lombard, profusely illustrated, wherein noted writer Busch brilliantly captures the
essense of the Lombard character. Busch would later go on
to great acclaim for his coverage of World War II from the
front lines.

063 Calhoun, Dorothy. "Carole Lombard's House Is a Back-
     ground for a Blonde." *Motion Picture*, May 1934, pp.
     40-41, 90-91.

An analysis, with 7 photos, of Carole's Hollywood
Boulevard "party house," decorated by William Haines to
match Lombard's hair color and personality. The house, as
pictured here, has remained virtually unchanged for the
past 50 years.

064 Carle, Teet. "Carole Lombard: Elegance in Action."
     Hollywood Studio, Oct. 1981, pp. 11-15.

Written by a former studio publicist, this piece--for
the most part--gives a standard rehash of known facts and
myths, which is disappointing since the author claims to
have seen and known Lombard during his studio tenure.

065 "Carole Lombard Betrays Herself." *Hollywood,* Jan.
     1937, pp. 34-35, 66.

Adequate representation of Lombard's character and
her animated home life. Gives a brief glimpse into her
career but the tone is so gossipy that any revelation is
lost. Mention is made of Margaret Tallichet and others
helped by Lombard.

066 "Carole Lombard Dies in Crash After Aiding U. S. De-
     fense Bond Campaign." *Life,* 26 Jan. 1942, p. 25.

Two paragraph description of Lombard's last day of
life and the plane crash that killed her. Includes a bond
rally photo from the Cadle Tabernacle in Indianapolis.

067 Crichton, Kyle. "Fun In Flickers." *Colliers,* 24
     Feb. 1940, pp. 11, 39-40.

More than many, this piece accurately pins down
Lombard's career and personality. Two cogent comments
about Carole: "What distinguishes her in Hollywood is her
genuineness. If she hates you, she lets the secret come
out. If she likes you, she'll battle cops all up and down
Hollywood Boulevard on your behalf." And, "Her new ambition is to get some sense into the profession [of movie-
making] by making it a sporting proposition. If they
think $150,000 is too much for her services, she'll gamble
with them on percentage, either cashing in big or standing
part of the losses." This would become standard practice
in Hollywood, but not for another decade. Also, it was in

this   article that Lombard supposedly railed   that   *Supernatural*'s director Victor Halperin ought to be running a
delicatessen instead of a motion picture production.

068 Cruikshank,   Herbert.   "Three-In-One Girl."   *Motion
     Picture*, Nov. 1930, pp. 74, 110.

     Cruikshank's article was the first to appear about
Lombard as a Paramount Player.   Written after her appearance in *Safety In Numbers* and before Carole had an e,   it
revealsl her to have already formed the hard shell of her
character; stating that her goal is to become a comedienne
who could still play drama on the order of *Rain,* that
Hollywood marriages can't work, and that money can't buy
happiness, "so to hell with it."   She mentions her mother
as the one who keeps her from "going Hollywood" in attitude, and recounts both her Fort Wayne background and the
auto accident.

069 *Current Biography*, 1942, p. 526-27.

     One paragraph biography followed by a magazine bibli-
ography.

070 "Death on Table Rock." *Newsweek,* 26 Jan. 1942, p. 26.

     Concentration here is on reaction to the   crash of
Flight 3, including charges by critics that the print
media had made Lombard's death seem more important than
the loss of 15 army pilots.   Logically enough, given her
national stature, it was.

071 Dickens, Homer.   "Carole Lombard: Her Comic Sense
     Derived from an Instinctual Realism."   *Films In
     Review,* Feb. 1961, pp. 70-86.

     A standard *FIR* career biography including 22 photos
and filmography.

072 Di Mambro, Dina. "Carole Lombard: Loveable Madcap."
     Hollywood Studio, Oct. 1983, pp. 8-11.

     Routine outline of her life, with 6 photos.

073 Doherty, Edward.   "Can the Gable-Lombard Love Story
     Have a Happy Ending?" *Photoplay,* May 1938, pp. 18-19.

     An analysis of the Gable-Lombard romance nearly a
year before their marriage, written at a time when their
future together was in doubt because Gable's second wife,
Ria Langham Gable, refused to grant him a divorce.

074 Dowling, Mark.   "A New Way to Men's Hearts--as told
     Carole Lombard." *Motion Picture,* July 1936, pp. 36,
     82.

The title refers to Carole's impassioned plea for the right of women to retain their individuality despite marriage. Lombard the early feminist said with conviction: "Independence eliminates almost all of the unpleasantness that can develop between a man and wife. The woman who works can't relax--can't stagnate. She'll remain the vivid, attractive, *awake* woman the man married... If I should marry again, I could find time to manage my home and be with my husband without interfering with my career. Right now I run my own house. I have pleasant, ample vacations. I find time for an interesting social life, seeing my friends, going where I choose. If marriage is difficult for an actress--and I believe it is difficult--it's for other reasons than the fact that an actress works."

075 Drexler, Rosalyn. "Looking for Lombard." New York *News Magazine*, 13 July 1975.

A 6 page tribute to Lombard including strangely inaccurate interview excerpts and photos. The cover of this issue is a large color photo of Lombard in a negligee; a second color photo is inside.

076 "End of a Mission." *Time*, 26 Jan. 1942, p. 17.

In a section labeled "Catastrophe," Lombard's bond tour and the crash of Flight 3 are detailed. *Time* said, "The blonde actress--who had often said she was glad she was not beautiful--in one day raised $2,000,000." Facts are delivered in straight-forward fashion, with no hint as to possible causes of the crash.

077 Factor, Max. "Give Yourself a Break In Beauty Says Carole Lombard." (Magazine unknown), Jan. 1935, pp. 41, 44.

Fluffy piece describing how the noted make-up man handles Lombard. Includes quotes by the star.

078 Fleming, William. "Perfect Abandon for Carole Lombard." *Shadowplay*, June 1934, pp. 30-31, 64-66.

No information available.

079 Fletcher, Adele Whitely. "How Clark Gable and Carole Lombard Live." *Photoplay*, Oct. 1940, pp. 30-32, 84.

An unusually accurate assessment of the Lombard-Gable home life, including background information on both and quotes from Carole's longtime cook Jessie, as well as Madalynne Fields, Alice Marble, "Teach" Tennant, and Harry Fleischmann. Includes many unusual photos of the Encino ranch.

080   French, William F.   "Be Modern or Be a Wallflower
       Says Carole Lombard." *Motion Picture*, Aug., 1935,
       pp. 28-29, 58.

An unorthodox article in which Lombard uncannily pre-
sages the liberated woman of a generation or more later.
In a day when women were largely restricted to cooking and
raising children, Carole insisted that the new breed of
woman must do more. "The up-to-date girl has a variety of
interests," she said.   "She rides, she drives, she plays
bridge, she reads, she follows the latest plays, she
studies, she goes in for sports with a zest. She doesn't
putter.   She never does things halfway.   She does things
with a will, never half-heartedly."

081   French, William F.   "Carole Lombard's Greatest Wish."
       Photoplay, April 1942, pp. 30, 69.

According to French, Lombard's greatest wish was that
she would die "in full bloom," and that she didn't want to
"just wait...and wilt." Carole had nothing publicly to
say about the death of Jean Harlow, so the quote French
reveals here becomes important as it reinforces Lombard's
own feelings about dying young. Published posthumously.
An eerie, fascinating piece.

082   Garceau, Jean and Inez Cocke.   "Dear Mr. G." *Ladies
       Home Journal*, July 1961, pp. 25+, August 1961, pp.
       42+, and Sept. 1961, pp. 66+.

Excerpted chapters from Garceau's affectionate Gable
biography.   The July issue is chapter one, describing the
period 1938-39 in Gable's life, including *GWTW*, marriage
to Lombard, and the purchase of the Encino ranch.

083   Goldbeck, Elizabeth.   Interview, *Motion Picture Clas-
       sic*, April 1931, pp. 73+.

No information available.

084   Goldbeck, Elizabeth.   "Bill Powell Talks About His
       Wife." *Movie Classic*, Nov. 1932, pp. 15, 68.

At the midpoint of their marriage, William Powell
here discusses the problems of his marriage, plus
Lombard's recent medical problems. Said Powell, "Someone
came down here the other day to take our pictures out in
the garden as 'Hollywood's happy couple'--one of the few
'lasting marriages' in Hollywood.   It makes you feel a
little self-conscious, posing for them--when you realize
that half the time in cases like that the divorce papers
are filed before the magazine even gets on the stands.
It's almost a challenge.   Marriage, itself, is dangerous
for that reason.   It professes to be able to control love.
It says, 'Now that you've said these words, you've got to

go on loving this man or this woman.' You chafe under it, naturally.

085   Hall, Gladys.   "Why I Married Bill Powell." *Motion Picture,* Dec. 1931, pp. 58-59, 99.

Details the wedding and Carole's supposed contentment with marriage.   Apparently, Lombard wasn't immune to unwanted advances from married men, even though her use of profanity might have partially been designed in this direction.   Hall says, "It doesn't make very pleasant hearing--Carole telling about the [married] men. One man, now a star, tried to--well, it took an electrician on the set to call off the dog." Of her new life with Mr. Powell, Carole spoke in remarkably unromantic terms: "Bill and I do, and intend to do, what we feel like doing, where and with whom. *But*--we both know what the other feels like doing, and why. That's all there is to it."

086   Hall, Gladys.   "There are 7 Kinds of Love." *Photoplay,* Oct. 1933, pp. 50-51, 99.

Lombard here reveals her early loves in cryptic fashion.   Among those referred to, although not directly, are Howard Hughes and Horace Liveright. Almost certainly speaking of Hughes she said, "And then, at last, I had to realize that the poor boy's feet were clay, wingless clay. So much so, that they had trampled my ideal right under them.   It took me a long time to learn that lesson because, of all loves, the love you create yourself is the hardest to kill, takes the longest time to die."

087   Hall,   Gladys.   "Lombard--As She Sees Herself." *Motion Picture,* Nov. 1938, pp. 34-35, 66, 68.

The best print interview of Lombard's life, in which Gladys Hall slowly opens up her subject to reveal the warmth and depth of the soul underneath. (Reprinted in Chapter 4).

088   Harrison, H.   "Sincerely, Carole Lombard." *Silver Screen,* July 1935, pp. 31+.

No information available.

089   Hartley, Katharine. "The Girl Who Is Always Starting Something." *Movie Mirror,* Jan. 1936, pp. 24-25, 76-77.

Focuses on the originality of Lombard as a personality, with several sanguine quotes.   Her unorthodoxy is covered through such examples as her off-beat parties, and her exhibitions of independence.   "I can't be bothered to clutter up my life with stardom gestures," said Lombard. "Like having a maid on the set...I'm not too lazy to light

my own cigarettes."   Later she said, "The same with
driving my own small car to the studio. All this liveried
chauffeur business, the big limousines--a *nuisance!*" As
soon as Carole did it, a trend was established among actresses. Then there was the case of Lombard and her make-
up tray, eliminating the fussing of make-up artists;   she
applied her own.   As for the hairstyle she adopted, "Curl
my bangs every two minutes?   I guess not. I'll wear them
straight.   Let the other girls fuss with theirs if they
want to.   Not me."   Spartan ideals like these did not en-
dear Lombard with the competition--other more pampered
ingenues.

090   Hastings, Dennison. "Clark Gable's Romantic Plight."
      Photoplay, Sept. 1936, pp. 12-13, 77.

      No information available.

091   "How Gable's Wives Made Him Great."   *Screen   Guide,*
      Nov. 1939, pp. 30-33.

      The theme of this photo-feature is stated in nice-
but-nasty ways like this: "No reflection on Gable is the
fact that his wives have helped him; each thought him a
wonderful man and naturally did all she could to promote
his interests." Earlier wives Josephine Dillon and Ria
Langham, both older and hardly glamorous in appearance,
are pictured to great disadvantage in a piece that casts a
dubious light on Gable.   Lombard is depicted in one full
page color photo with Gable plus two other candids.   No
enlightening text regarding Carole is included.

092   Hunt, Julie Lang.   "How Carole Lombard Plans a
      Party." *Photoplay,* Feb. 1935, pp. 67, 94-95.

      A detailed primer on bash-throwing, with many tips
from the acknowledged queen of hostesses.   Astounding ob-
servations like this one abound: "'The zero hour for any
dinner,' Carole told me, 'arrives along with the coffee
and brandy.   At that moment even a party that has started
off at a rollicking pace can and will curl up and die, unless the hostess is on her toes.'"

093   Hunt, Julie Lang.   "The Utterly Balmy Home Life of
      Carole Lombard." *Motion Picture,* Feb. 1937, pp. 36+.

      A description of life at Carole's Bel Air home, a
place that included Fieldsie, hired help, and a variety of
pets, all apparently just escaped from a Marx Brothers
movie. An entertaining piece.

094   Kathryn. "Letters of a Movie Fan in Hollywood."
      Movie Mirror, Sept. 1933, pp. 62-63, 92-93.

      Gimmicky article written in the style of a letter

from one fan to another. Details the social side of
Lombard along with her thoughts on health and beauty.

095 Keene, D. "Carole Gets Her Own Way." *Silver Screen*,
     May, 1934, pp. 30+.

     No information available.

096 "Keeping Up with Hollywood." *Woman's Home Companion*,
     Dec. 1940, p. 15.

     An extremely brief biographical sketch accompanied by
a candid color photo. The text concludes with, "Carole is
known as Hollywood's best-dressed woman...shrewdly manages
her own business affairs...plans to become a producer."

097 Lane, Virginia. "How Carole Lombard's Clothes Match
     Her Moods." *Movie Classic*, Sept. 1935, pp. 44-45,
     64-65, 75.

     A routine publicity piece that ends up praising the
starlet's figure and taste. Interesting only because the
quotes are not by Lombard but rather by her close friend,
designer Travis Banton.

098 Lee, Rosemary. "The Tragic Love Story of Dorothy
     Dell and Russ Columbo." *Movies*, Nov. 1934, pp. 14-
     14, 32.

     Lombard is barely mentioned in this florid account of
the Columbo and Dell tragedies. In a historical sense,
some writers failed to connect Columbo with Lombard and in
fact, their relationship was not widely known outside
Hollywood circles.

099 Lee, Sonia. "Carole Lombard Tells Why Hollywood Mar-
     riages Can't Succeed." *Motion Picture*, May 1934, pp.
     28-29, 80.

     Title tells all as Carole explains why her relation-
ship with Bill Powell failed.

100 Lee, Sonia. "Carole Lombard Reborn." *Movie Mirror*,
     July 1934, pp. 26-27, 81.

     Written after the completion of *Twentieth Century*,
this piece details the state of her career and personal
life. Conspicuous by its absense is the name Russ
Columbo, although Carole does expound on the reasons for
her failed marriage, and her ambition to reach "the peak"
of movie stardom.

101 Lee, Sonia. "We Would Have Married--." *Movie Clas-
     sic*, Dec. 1934, pp. 37, 66.

The story of Lombard and Columbo emerges here through quotes by Carole on a topic that was never one of her favorites: her fiance's shocking death. This article is a rare one, perhaps the only time in her life she opened up on the subject, and has apparently been overlooked by her biographers.   Otherwise, there certainly would have been extensive analysis of her claim that she spent three frightful weeks knowing that Russ Columbo's "number was up," and that something terrible would happen to him.   "I believe that everything that happens is determined by an inflexible Fate," said Lombard.   "I believe that Russ's death was pre-destined.   And I am glad that it came when he was so happy--so happy in our love and in his winning of stardom."

102   Lee, Sonia.   "What Carole Lombard Knows About Men." *Screen Play*, Feb. 1935, pp. 16-17, 63.

Lombard muses philosophically about relationships and marriage, stating her idea of the perfect marriage, and alluding to her first love (probably Howard Hughes) and her life with William Powell.

103   Lee, Sonia. "Self-Made Woman." *Movie Classic*, Dec. 1935, pp. 32+.

No information available.

104   Leisen, Mitchell.   "The Lowdown on Lombard."   *Film Weekly*, 10 July 1937.

A behind the scenes look at Lombard by her close friend and oft-times director.   Among the let's-call-a-spade quotes: "She's over-modest about her own capabilities, and never wants to tackle a part she isn't certain she can do." And as for Lombard being a beautiful woman who can also act, Leisen says, "...Carole's no beauty, with her high forehead, big mouth and heavy jaw. What she has got is the right combination of personality, intelligence, humor, feeling and enthusiasm." Interesting trivia: Leisen and Lombard were both born on October 6, making them kindred spirits--sensitive, generous, narcissistic Librans.

105   Liza.   "Lombard, Then and Now." *Screenland*, Nov. or Dec. 1937, pp. 30-31, 77.

Contrasts Lombard's first stint at the Pathe Studios in Culver City, then her return there 9 years later after it had become Selznick International.   Includes facts about her Pathe films and career.

106   "Lombard and Laughton View Their New Film and Find It Exciting." *Life*, 30 Sept. 1940, pp. 47-50.

Interesting   concept: putting   photographer   Peter
Stackpole   beneath   the   movie   screen   during   a   special
screening   of *They   Knew   What   They   Wanted* for Lombard,
Garson Kanin,   and Charles Laughton.   The result is a candid look at all three,   illuminated by Kanin's later book
Hollywood that chronicled his own love for--and Laughton's
hatred of--Lombard.   Here,   with the pressure of filming
over, all are pals.   11 photos and captions included, plus
brief text.

107 "The Love Story of Carole Lombard and Clark Gable."
     Look, 11 May 1937, pp. 34-41.

The first and therefore the most remarkable   feature
on the deepening Lombard-Gable romance.   27 photos   with
descriptive captions.   Among these are startling (for
their day) stills taken for *Dynamite* showing a bare-
breasted Lombard,   plus another early cheesecake shot of
her derriere.   Most important of the photos is one showing
her facial scar that nearly led to a lawsuit.

108 Madden, George.   "Hollywood   Is Ruled   by   Women."
     Movie Mirror, Nov. 1934, pp. 46-47, 77.

This excellent example of a feminist Lombard includes
her views on the working woman and marriage as an evolving
institution.   "I   think   it will be the men who   have   to
change their attitude toward wives," said Carole.   "At all
events, it seems absurd and illogical that a two-fifty li-
cense gives a man and woman the privilege of legally living together,   while divorce costs five hundred dollars to
give   them   the   privilege   of   living   apart."   She   also
stated, "Look about you and you will see for the first
time since the ancient rule of the Amazons, a colony of
economically independent women.   Here they are, rulers of
a   fantastic kingdom where the wealth is a product of   the
women.   Contrast such a state with other times.   Women in
kitchens, subservient, mental and physical slaves.   A roof
over   their   heads and food for   their   stomachs--provided
they   could   please   some   man   enough   to   share   him   in
marriage...With all that went the so-called double standard of morals, a standard contrived by the lordly   male.
Well,   Hollywood,   with women emancipated from   masculine
domination, is changing that.   A new moral code, perhaps--
at all events a different social order brought   about   by
economic independence."

109 Madden, George. "The Evolution of a Wow." *Movie Mir-*
     ror, Dec. 1936, pp. 48-49, 100-101.

Lombard   reflects on having "arrived" as   an   actress
and a star in the wake of *My Man Godfrey.*   She   candidly
admits   to   having previously flopped through film after
film,   while having no idea of what she was doing.   Of her
first five years on-screen she said, "I merely stood there

in front of the camera and did what the director told me,
and tried to keep my mind blank so I wouldn't interfere
with his thought transmission.   Something seemed to give
forth on the screen, but I never knew how it happened.   It
was all an accident." Of John Barrymore she stated, "It
would take a book to cover all the things he did to help.
But perhaps the greatest was the subtle way he built my
self-confidence and flattered me into believing I was
good."   Among her most revealing statements is this one:
"For ten years I've been the only person in Hollywood who
believed in me, except, perhaps Pushface Lombard--who is a
Pekingese."

110   Maddox, Ben.   "The Real Low-down on Lombard."
      Picture Play, Nov. 1937, pp. 16-17, 88.

      Indifferent interview with Lombard touching on rumors
surrounding her relationship with Gable, and her practical
nature.   Maddox makes no effort to look beneath the surface of his subject.

111   Maddox, Ben.   "Why Lombard Won't Talk." *Photoplay,*
      Feb. 1938, pp. 14-15, 76.

      Maddox states at the beginning that Carole has re-
fused to grant interviews, then postulates on the reasons
why. Basically a rehash of old information.

112   Manners, M. J. "Killed In Action." *Silver Screen,*
      April, 1942, p. 22.

      No information available.

113   Matthews, Francis Barr. "The Story Behind Russ Colum-
      bo's Death." *Movie Mirror,* Nov. 1934, pp. 65, 80.

      This brief Columbo biography goes farther than most
in acknowledging a Lombard-Columbo relationship.   "He
hoped to marry her," said Matthews.   "For a time he was
seen with Sally Blane, but in recent weeks he and Carole
had become more and more fond of each other until Hollywood expected the announcement of their engagement at any
moment."

114   McCarthy, Joe.   "The Five Wives of Clark Gable."
      Look, 18 Oct. 1955, pp. 103-114.

      A very standard regurgitation of the Lombard-Gable
romance and marriage.

115   McFee, Frederick. "Why Is Carole Lombard Hiding Out
      from Hollywood?" *Screen Book,* Oct. 1938, pp. 28, 57-
      58.

      One of the most insightful of Lombard articles uncovering many of the good deeds she performed and tried to keep quiet for fear people would consider them publicity stunts. (Reprinted in Chapter 4).

116   "Movie of the Week: *Nothing Sacred*." *Life,* 6 Dec. 1937, pp. 36-39.

     Describes the film's plot in pictures with captions. Also gives a promotional look at director William Wellman. 24 photos in all, plus brief text.

117   Obituary. *Time,* 26 Jan. 1942, p. 76.

     One paragraph summary of Lombard's life and career.

118   O'Malley, Agnes. "Scars That Glorified." *Motion Picture Classic,* June 1929, pp. 45, 92.

     Written more than three years after her near-tragic auto accident, this short piece alludes to the serious nature of her rehabilitation. "Carol lay in bed for eight months," wrote O'Malley, "under the care of a skillful surgeon. Most of this time she spent strapped to the mattress to prevent the slightest movement which would jar the surgeon's delicate work. The days were long and dreary...And the surgeon worked on patiently and painstakingly. When the stitches were removed from her face, he came daily for months to massage the scars with olive oil."

119   Pringle, Henry F. "Mr. and Mrs. Clark Gable." *Ladies Home Journal,* May 1940, pp. 20, 99.

     A celebration of the Lombard-Gable romance that describes their income, home life, and Carole's sense of humor.

120   Ramsey, Walter. "Ex-Bachelor." *Modern Screen,* (month unknown) 1932, pp. 31, 121.

     William Powell's perspective on his attraction to Carole Lombard, and his thoughts on their marriage.

121   Romayne. "A Letter to Heaven." *Screenland,* March 1942, pp. 32-33, 86-88.

     A tribute to Lombard by the secretary of director Wesley Ruggles. One of the pieces, published shortly after her death, that embellished her legend without caring a great deal about the authenticity of the *facts* and anecdotes presented.

122   St. Johns, Adela Rogers. "A Gallant Lady...Carole Lombard." *Liberty,* 28 Feb. 1942, pp. 21-24+.

An analysis of what made Carole tick, published soon after her death. One of the longest, most thoughtful pieces written about Lombard, it dissects her in terms of relationships (Fieldsie and Columbo are used as examples) and spiritual beliefs. Of the concept of God, St. Johns quotes the following from Lombard: "I don't seem to get solemn about it and some people might not understand. That's why I never talk about it. I think it's all here-- in the mountains and the desert. I don't think God is a softie, either. In the end it's better if people are forced back into--well--into being right, before they're too far gone. I think your temple is your everyday living."

123 Samuels, Charles. "Clark Gable and the Women Who Loved Him." *Good Housekeeping,* Nov. 1961, pp. 68-69, 220-240, 246-250.

The second part of a condensation of Samuels' book, *The King: the Story of Clark Gable.* This section deals extensively, and mostly accurately, with the Lombard-Gable relationship, Carole's death, and Clark's reaction to it.

124 Schrott, E. "Hollywood's Goofy Gal Goes Glamorous." *Screen Book,* Feb. 1939, pp. 28+.

No information available.

125 "Secret Heartbreak of William Powell." *True Experiences,* June 1938, pp. 17-20, 48-50.

Maudlin, detailed look at Powell's relationships with Lombard and Jean Harlow, how he lost one to divorce and the other to death, and how he couldn't cope with these setbacks.

126 Service, F. Interview. *Movie Classic,* May 1933, pp. 51+.

No information available.

127 Seymore, Hart. "Carole Lombard Tells: 'How I Live by a Man's Code." *Photoplay,* June 1937, pp. 12-13, 78.

In this interview, Carole lists 10 enlightening tips on how to thrive in a "man's world." Lombard the feminist strikes again, proclaiming, "A woman has just as much right in this world as a man, and can get along in it just as well if she puts her mind to it."

128 Smalley, Jack. "Lombard Creates a Glamorous Rival." *Movie Mirror,* March 1937, pp. 58-59, 72.

A detailed account of Lombard's altruistic sponsor-

ship, then going at full speed, of aspiring actress Margaret Tallichet, known to Carole as "Tally." Carole said,
"Something about her struck me as unusual. Her personality, rather than any exceptional beauty. Bright mind, too,
and that's important. I had the sudden hunch that this
girl, if given a little help, might go places." Tallichet
went on to a few screen appearances before marrying director William Wyler and retiring from the screen.

129   Street, James. "Two Happy People." *Movie and Radio
      Guide,* 27 April, 4 May, 11 May 1940.

A three part article, one of countless published at
this time, detailing the Lombard-Gable marriage and their
Encino ranch. No memorable disclosures are included.

130   Sylvia. "How Sylvia Changed 'Carole of the Curves'
      to Svelt Carole Lombard." *Photoplay,* April 1933, pp.
      50-51, 80-81.

The noted physical culturist and masseuse recounts
her work on Lombard, changing the roly-poly Sennett girl
into a glamour queen.

131   Thompson, Morton. "Practical Joker's Paradise."
      Cosmopolitan, March 1946, pp. 58-59, 138-140.

Thompson states that at one of Carole's parties, she
wired the powder room for sound and proceeded to play re-
cordings of actresses' backstabbing of one another as the
evening's finale. This forms one anecdote in an examination of the humor of various celebrities.

132   Underhill, D. "Homemaker Lombard." *Screen Book,*
      Nov. 1939, pp. 52+.

No information available.

133   Van Slyke, Helen. "Five Days with Lombard and Gable."
      The Saturday Evening Post, Nov. 1975, pp. 49-51, 101,
      106.

Served up as promotion for the film *Gable and
Lombard.* As with the motion picture it trumpets, any
relation between this article and the truth about Lombard
and Gable is purely coincidental.

134   Waterbury, Ruth. "What the Loss of Carole Lombard
      Means to Clark Gable." *Photoplay,* April 1942, pp.
      28-30, 68-69.

An account of the plane crash from Gable's perspective. It appears fluffy on the surface but offers a look
at Gable's actions following the tragedy, plus a recap of
their marriage.

135 Williams, Whitney. "Hollywood's Most Shocking Woman."
     Screen Book, May 1934, pp. 28, 77.

     An overview of Lombard's unabashed social personali-
ty; includes no direct quotes.

136 Williams, Whitney.   "Hazing: a Short Story of the
     Initiation of Carole Lombard." *Silver Screen,* Sept.
     1937, p. 53.

     Trivial recounting of Lombard's first experience with
location work, with Buck Jones in Arizona.

137 Wilson, Elizabeth.   "That Funny Divorce."   *Silver
     Screen,* April 1934, pp. 18-19, 66.

     Chronicles the ongoing, post-divorce friendship of
Lombard and Powell, with an emphasis on Lombard's zany
parties.   Written just prior to the filming of *Twentieth
Century.*

138 Wilson, Elizabeth.   "Garbo Versus Lombard." *Silver
     Screen,* Dec. 1934, pp. 16+.

     No information available.

139 Wilson, Elizabeth.   "Tripping to New York." *Silver
     Screen,* April 1935, pp. 18+.

     No information available.

140 Wilson, Elizabeth.   "Merrily She Rolls   Along."
     Screenland, Oct. 1935, pp. 20-21, 85-86.

     Wilson, one of Lombard's closest columnist pals, de-
tails her relationship with the star at the time Carole
leased her "party house." A cut above most profiles, putting the unorthodox Lombard personality in perspective.

141 Wilson, Elizabeth. "Everything Has Been Done Before."
     Silver Screen, Jan. 1936, pp. 18-19, 57.

     Wilson's refreshingly honest style illuminates an
article about a visit to Carole's Hollywood Boulevard home
for an interview.   Wilson couldn't come up with an angle,
and Lombard gave her a typically, ribbingly hard time, as
did Fieldsie acting as secretary/domestic help. Elizabeth
Wilson's articles provide a rare look at the real Carole
Lombard, the way she lived her life and interacted with
the world, day to day. This piece is typically excellent.
Here is an example, as Wilson is sitting in Carole's home,
waiting for the star: "There was a clippity cloppity
sound which turned out to be La Lombard making a down-the-
stairs entrance in a pair of mules. And a very good looking pair of pajamas I might add.   With a few understate-

ments about my ability as a writer, Carole dropped onto
her best tufted sofa, as only Carole can drop, lit a cigarette and gave out, "Now this is going to be fun.   Miss
Wilson is about to spring an idea on us, though personally
I don't think she has had an idea in years.   Fieldsie,
better bring in some knick-knacks for her to chew on or
she'll want to stay to dinner." Referring to Carole as
"La Lombard" became a Wilson trademark.

142 Wilson, Elizabeth. "Carole and Bill Together Again!"
     Screenland, July 1936, pp. 20-21, 80-81.

     Lombard's pal Wilson visits the set of *My Man Godfrey*
(during filming of the scavenger hunt finale) and reports
on the goings-on. Trivial but entertaining piece.

143 Wilson, Elizabeth. "Projections: Carole Lombard."
     Silver Screen, Jan. 1937, pp. 22-23, 74-75.

     Describes Lombard as hostess during a recent trip to
New York; gives a (for Wilson) disappointingly inaccurate
recap of Carole's life and career; insights do emerge after a slow start.   Of Lombard's latest film (*Swing High,
Swing Low*) Wilson reports: "'It's my come-back picture,'
Carole will tell you.   Every picture Carole makes is her
'come-back' picture.   She discusses her 'return to the
screen' as if she had been off it for years." From here,
Wilson gets personal: "Carole, as her best friends will
gladly tell you, has many faults.   It seems that she
simply will not close drawers.   Dresser drawers, dressing
table drawers, bathroom cabinet drawers, they are all
hanging out at a rakish angle when Carole leaves for the
studio...Another of Carole's bad habits is to bite off the
edges of stationery while she is thinking what to write in
a letter.   She always writes with green ink, and her
spelling is something to lift an eyebrow over.   Her most
annoying little trick, though, is to change her hand-
writing when she is signing checks, and the bank clerks
used to go stark staring mad trying to figure out which
was Carole's signature and which was a forgery...If you
ever want to torture Miss Lombard...just stand near her
when she is under a hair dryer and carry on a conversation
with some one.   As a matter of fact you don't have to
talk, just move your lips, and laugh occasionally. Carole
will stand it as long as she can and then, dying with
curiosity, she will pop her head out from under the
roaring dryer and demand, 'What did you say?'   She has
just a little more than her normal share of curiosity."

144 Wilson, Elizabeth. Interview. *Screenland*, May 1940,
     pp. 26-27, 91.

     Answers rumors that said Carole was seriously ill
when in actuality she had just returned from a quail hunting trip with Gable.

145 Wilson, Elizabeth.   "It Looked Good for a Laugh   at
     Time." *Silver Screen,* Jan. 1941, pp. 26+.

No information available.

146 Wilson, Elizabeth. "What About Those Lombard Rumors?"
     Silver Screen, March 1942, pp. 26-27, 62-63.

     In conjunction with the release of *To Be or Not to
Be,* Wilson issued a defense of Lombard as regarded all the
rumors concerning: her imminent divorce from Gable;   her
imminent retirement from the screen; and her imminent
death from various health problems.   Only the marital rumors held possibilities, in retrospect. This article had
just gone .to press when Lombard died.

147 Worth, Don.   "Will Carole Lombard's Marriage End Her
     Career?" *Motion Picture,* July 1939, pp. 23, 56-57.

     An arm's length account of the Lombard-Gable wedding
composed of speculation and devoid of substance.

148 Zeitlin, Ida.   "At Home with the Gables."   *Picture
     Play,* Aug. 1940, pp. 20-21, 79-80.

     A look at the Lombard-Gable marriage from the angle
of their famous ranch in Encino.

FILM PORTRAYALS

149 *Gable: the King Remembered.*   A Jack Haley Jr. Pro-
     duction, 1975.   44 minutes.   Narrated by Peter
     Lawford.

     A video profile of Gable seen frequently on PBS.
Rare footage of Lombard includes their March, 1939 post-
wedding press conference in Bel Air, the Atlanta and Hollywood premieres of *GWTW,* Lombard's Indianapolis bond
tour, and the wreckage of the DC-3. William Wellman, interviewed by Lawford, states that because of Carole's
death, "To me, Gable is the most tragic man that the
motion picture business has ever had...Gable looked at
this woman with a love that I've never seen in my life."
Wellman also tells anecdotes about Lombard, including the
one about Carole wearing an evening gown and falling into
Fred MacMurray's pool, then proceeding to change into a
pair of Fred's pajamas and going right on with the party.

150 *Gable and Lombard.*   Universal, 1976.   131 minutes.

     An overwhelmingly fictionalized account of the rela-
tionship of the two stars that unfortunately stands as the
biggest boxoffice bomb of the 1970s. James Brolin and
Jill Clayburgh were badly miscast in the lead roles, with

Lombard portrayed as a foul-mouthed humorless brat and Gable a dim-witted hayseed. To this day, the way of *Gable and Lombard* blocks other film and book projects related to Carole Lombard.

151 *Malice in Wonderland.*   CBS-TV, 1985.   100 minutes.

Based on George Eels' book, *Hedda and Louella.*   Hedda Hopper is played by Jane Alexander, while Elizabeth Taylor does a hatchet-job on her own character, Louella Parsons in a TV-movie that emerges as a sub-par interpretation of their famous rivalry. Carole Lombard is portrayed in a bit part by then-unknown Denise Crosby, who would go on to notoriety as Lt. Tasha Yar on the Fox network series *Star Trek: the Next Generation.* As presented here, Lombard is childish, bitchy, and masculine. No feel for the real character is attempted.

152 *Our World*--Gone With the Wind: *the Making of a Classic--1939.* ABC-TV, 1987. 48 minutes. Hosted by Ray Gandolf and Linda Ellerbee.

This excellent but short-lived hour-long documentary series devoted an episode to the production of *GWTW.* In the process, dynamic Marcella Rabwin, who worked as David Selznick's executive assistant, gives a previously unknown, complicated account of how Gable came to play Rhett Butler against his will as a result of the triangle he formed with Lombard and his estranged second wife Ria. According to Rabwin, Clark wanted to marry Carole but Ria refused to divorce him, which became the key to forcing Gable into a part he didn't want: Clark was desperately in love with Carole Lombard, and so the only way he would ever say 'yes' [to *GWTW*] was through the divinations of Mr. L. B. Mayer, who said to his wife [Ria], 'If you will divorce Clark, we'll give you a half a million dollars'--which was more money than she had ever heard of in her life--'provided that you get Clark to play the part.' So in order to get the $500,000 she not only agreed to the divorce but told Clark she would give it to him only on the condition that he play this role. That's how we finally got Gable; a very reluctant Gable."

153 *Power Profiles, the Legendary Ladies: Carole Lombard.* A Richard Gabourie Presentation, 1985. 24 minutes.

A solid video portrait of Lombard that includes scarce footage such as scenes from her silent films, candids of Lombard and Powell (and Lombard and Gable) at Santa Anita, color home movies of a hunting trip with Clark, the bond tour, and out-takes from *My Man Godfrey.* Other subjects of *Power Profiles* include Gary Cooper and boxer Joe Louis.

154   *The Scarlett O'Hara War*.   NBC-TV, 1980.   105 minutes.

Tony   Curtis's portrayal of David O.   Selznick   highlights   a feast for fans of *Gone With the Wind* and classic
cinema in general.   Taken from Garson Kanin's   bestseller
Moviola,   this   TV movie chronicles the scheming and   mis-
adventures   of those actresses,   Carole Lombard   included,
who   tried   to land the role of Scarlett   O'Hara.   Sharon
Gless   makes an interesting Lombard in the   most   accurate
and   sincere   attempt   at   dramatizing   the   character   of
Lombard to date.

Appendix:
Archives and Holdings

When tracking down information on Carole Lombard or any star of the Golden Era, the trail inevitably begins at the Margaret Herrick Library of the Academy of Motion Picture Arts and Sciences in Beverly Hills, California. Their Lombard holdings include a still file and a microfiche biography file as well as a large inventory of rare movie magazines and as complete a film book collection as exists. The National Film Information Service serves as the link between the Margaret Herrick Library and film researchers around the country.

Many other libraries serve the student of motion picture history. The U. C. L. A. libraries contain, among others, the collections of Russell Birdwell, Cecil B. DeMille, Charles Laughton, Jack Benny, and Universal Studios. The U. S. C. libraries contain the collections of Burns and Allen, William Farnum, and Louella Parsons. In addition, the De Forest Research Service in Los Angeles maintains a library of over 5,000 books and related film material for use by scholars.

The Library of Congress in Washington is an obvious goldmine of film history information owing to its massive holdings. The New York Public Library is the repository for information on MGM, Paramount, and Universal Studios. The Museum of Modern Art's Study Center of the Department of Film in New York City maintains an outstanding collection related to motion pictures, as does the Wisconsin Center for Theatre Research in Madison.

Index

About the Author

ROBERT D. MATZEN, a freelance writer, is the author of *Research Made Easy: A Guide for Students and Writers.* He contributed the introduction to *Warren's Movie Poster Price Guide* and his articles have appeared in *Hollywood Studio, Movie Collector's World,* and *Goldmine.*